SUCCEED
THE SANDLER WAY

SUCCEED
THE SANDLER WAY

14 Personal and Professional Breakthroughs

KARL SCHEIBLE & ADAM BOYD

Sandler Training

Paperback ISBN: 978-0-692-55795-2
E-book: ISBN: 978-0-692-55796-9

*My dedication is to my parents and
C.S. "Chic" Lewis for all of their support.*

*I want to acknowledge the Sandler network
for the role they all played in my professional sales
development over the last 11 years.*

—KARL SCHEIBLE

To Erin.

*And thank you to Karl,
who gave me a shot seven years ago
and has supported me ever since.*

—ADAM BOYD

CONTENTS

FOREWORD

For as long as we have been delivering training, Sandler® trainers have been on the receiving end of unprompted, unsolicited comments like these:

- "The Sandler training had a positive impact on my entire life, not just on my income."
- "This didn't just change my sales performance. It changed the way I interacted with my family, and it improved my life at home."
- "Not only did the Sandler principles change the way I communicated with prospects and customers, they improved my relationships with everyone else, including the people with whom I worked."

These kinds of personal transformations bring home a core truth about the system devised by our founder, David Sandler.

Ultimately, implementing the Sandler Selling System isn't just about becoming a better salesperson. It's about becoming a better person, period.

Successfully training salespeople in the Sandler methodology inevitably means helping them to bring about their own breakthroughs, breakthroughs that end up affecting multiple areas of their lives. All of us who have conducted training sessions have seen, first hand, transformative experiences that took our participants well beyond the realm of explosive growth in prospecting, qualifying and closing, and created new possibilities for growth in many areas. All of us have been moved by those stories.

For some time, we've been considering the possibility of collecting into a single volume a number of these accounts—stories that focused not just on the sales numbers, but also on the human dimension. When Karl Scheible and Adam Boyd approached us about such a project, it was easy to say, "yes!"

What you will find between these covers is not only a remarkable testament to the effectiveness of the Sandler Selling System® methodology, but also a ringing endorsement of the enduring impact of these two Sandler trainers. They have shown us all, not only through their clients' examples, but also through their own, what it truly means to succeed the Sandler way.

David H. Mattson
President/CEO, Sandler Training

INTRODUCTION

Congratulations on choosing to open this book. Perhaps you bought it yourself, or perhaps someone who cares about you gave it to you. Whatever the case, you have a desire to succeed. Before you start reading, we would like to set some clear expectations and discuss the choices that you will be facing when you finish.

True success, we believe, comes to those who strive to overcome not just external challenges but internal ones as well. Creating these internal "breakthroughs" sets you on the path to the most meaningful successes, not only in sales, but in other areas of your life if you so choose. In the pages that follow, we'll be sharing true stories with you about people who've done exactly that—including ourselves. The guiding principle for creating a breakthrough is deceptively simple-sounding: Be candid with yourself. We have been brutally honest about our own fears and flaws, and so have the people we've interviewed. Taking a good, hard look at yourself is a prerequisite of any breakthrough. Only by clearly seeing where you are now can you break through to where you want to be.

We realize it's possible that you picked up this book because you recognized the name "Sandler Training"—and if that's the case, the odds are good that you sell for a living or work with someone who does. If you are like most of the salespeople we work with, you are eager to create a financial breakthrough. We're willing to bet, though, that you also feel a level of discomfort with certain aspects of selling. Cold calls may seem intimidating. Perhaps you find it easy to talk to low-level clients, but you are hesitant about calling on the C-level. Maybe you have trouble discussing money, dealing with resistance at the close or conveying value in the face of intense competition.

Many salespeople don't know how to deal with such challenges. They're afraid to admit that they're deeply uneasy about these situations. Usually, they choose to "tough it out" until they change companies, hoping for some relief; then, they take their negative habits and attitudes to the next job. Some salespeople tolerate this kind of discomfort for their entire careers, blaming outside forces like "the economy" or "my boss" for the quality of their lives. They don't reach a point where they say to themselves, "You know what? I've had enough. Something has to change, and the change starts with me."

This book contains a series of first-person interviews with salespeople, sales managers and CEOs who have had enough.

All the professionals we interviewed decided that it was not external circumstances but their own self-limiting beliefs that were keeping them from realizing their dreams and aspirations. If this book does its job, you will reach the same conclusion—and take effective action on that life-changing discovery.

IF YOU DECIDE TO KEEP READING, HERE IS OUR REQUEST

Please take your time and read every chapter carefully. Look for the similarities in the breakthrough stories for each person. Note the chapters that most resonate with you, and read them as often as necessary. Have your favorite method of taking notes handy, so you can jot down ideas as you go.

If some of the stories make you uncomfortable, be encouraged. That's a sign that you've encountered an experience that's relevant to your world. Keep reading. Be willing to move outside of your comfort zone.

The people in this book were not "natural-born salespeople." In fact, all of them were quite the opposite. What they have in common is purpose and vision, along with the desire and commitment to make constructive changes. All of them reached a point in their careers where they knew deep down that "getting by" was not working for them.

If you're still reading, we're assuming that you know that, too—and are willing to take action on what you know.

COMMON THEMES

You'll see some common themes in all of these breakthrough artists. First, they realized that they had internal beliefs that were negatively impacting their behaviors on sales calls or other professional situations. Next, they admitted the severity of the financial consequences that those beliefs were causing. Then they worked hard to create an inventory of new beliefs that were more productive, and finally they persevered to put those beliefs into practice, even though it was uncomfortable at first. Over time, they gradually replaced self-defeating attitudes with ones that led to positive actions.

In each and every case, the results were amazing, both financially and on a personal level.

ABOUT SANDLER TRAINING

Sandler Training delivers over 450,000 hours of sales and sales management training each year. That means that, conservatively, the Sandler network coaches and trains upwards of 20,000 people a year. The vast majority of the people who attend a Sandler program love what we share with them and put it into action. However, not everyone fully adopts the attitudes, techniques and behaviors that we teach. To be honest, this is the most disappointing part of our job. We want as many people as possible to break through so they are selling stress-free, making more money and achieving their goals. That's why we wrote this book.

The results that are shared here are not meant to highlight our particular training center and clients as being somehow special. We are only one out of over 250 Sandler Training® centers worldwide. We are only two trainers out of close to 700 around the world. These results are indicative of the results delivered by the entire Sandler network.

Once you finish this book, you will have two choices. You can put it on a shelf and keep selling the way you are today and get the same results. Or you can seek out a Sandler trainer in your city, a professional who is ready, willing and able to help you to break through the Sandler way, and take the next step on the success journey.

—Karl Scheible and Adam Boyd

PART ONE

Breaking Point or Turning Point?

I n this part of the book, we will each share our own stories of personal and professional breakthroughs using the Sandler principles. Neither of us consider ourselves to be a "natural-born" salesperson. We surely weren't running around when we were little kids yelling, "Look at me, I'm a salesperson!" while all of our friends pretended to be firemen or astronauts.

When you read our stories, you'll see that we both were weak in sales. In fact, we now know that we were so weak early in our careers that there was no chance that we could have made it to where we are now without the help of our peers in the Sandler network, our coaches and the volumes of Sandler reinforcement material we devoured. If we can make it, you can make it. We could never have written a plausible book about breakthroughs if we hadn't committed to the process of creating them in our own lives.

CHAPTER 1

Closing the Best Deal of All

KARL SCHEIBLE

My very first memory of sales is as a nine-year-old kid, selling candy for the YMCA.

My dad worked out a simple script for me and had me memorize it. I can still recite it verbatim 43 years later. My father is a very successful businessman who pushed my siblings and me to succeed in everything we did. Failure was not in his vocabulary. He drilled me on the behavior needed to succeed as a candy salesperson and sent me out the door with the rallying cry, "You will sell more than anybody!"

> *"Luck is preparation meeting opportunity."* —David Sandler

I sold so much candy going door to door to both homes and businesses that eventually the YMCA could not provide me with any more inventory to sell. I sold almost as much as the rest of the membership combined. Was I a competent salesperson? Not really. I had a number of special circumstances in my favor. I was selling something that people wanted, at a low price, and they were supporting a good cause. How many people will reject a young kid from the YMCA who's only asking for a dollar?

This early sales experience taught me something I could only understand in hindsight. In spite of all the *yeses* my pitch received, I recall one vivid *no*. I belonged to the Maplewood branch of the YMCA, a branch located in our city. While I was delivering my pitch to a woman way out in the suburbs, she asked, "What branch of the Y do you belong to?" I thought for a moment and then said, "Greece," a suburban branch, believing she would not want to support the inner-city branch. Quickly and sternly, she said, "No!" and slammed the door.

Walking down the driveway, my head down with rejection, I noticed my nametag: "Karl Scheible, Maplewood YMCA." I still recall the embarrassment and guilt I felt. It was the last time that I ever lied on a sales call. Here I was a nine-year-old salesperson— and my instinct was to lie! Of course, my intent was not to deceive but to give an answer that I thought the prospect wanted to hear. In retrospect, I realize this was an early warning sign of my deep-seated need for approval.

BEYOND THE PAPER ROUTE

High school provided my next selling experience. I wanted to attend a private school, St. Thomas Aquinas. My dad, who had attended Aquinas, sat me down the summer before my first year and said that if I wanted to go to that school, I would have to pay my own way. After all, that was what he had done. I protested, "Are you kidding me? My paper route won't cover that!" Back in 1975, the $800 tuition was a lot of money. Fortunately, my dad had a plan. He always had a plan. He said that he would help me set up a business producing and selling notebook and paper products for my fellow students. Printing was a natural for me. I was a fourth-generation printer and I grew up in the craft. That summer, I opened shop within my dad's printing company and started to print notebook paper. I also printed jobs like tickets, stationery and flyers for small businesses.

One day in ninth grade, while selling paper out of my locker, I received a summons to the dean's office. When I got there, the dean of students proceeded to reprimand me for selling something that "competed" with the school bookstore, even though my product was of a higher quality. My eyes welled up as I explained that I had to pay my way through school and that I needed the business. Fortunately, the school respected entrepreneurship. They started to give me some of their small printing jobs. I eventually was handling most of their printing needs: their stationery, tickets and brochures. Business grew to the point that I had to borrow $5,000 from my grandmother to buy additional equipment.

Necessity, fear and desperation can be great motivators. I wanted to attend Aquinas badly enough to stand my ground when confronted by the dean—and I won his support. If I hadn't done that, I'm not sure how I would have made it through school.

I maintained the printing business into college, until I dropped out at the end of my second year. Actually, I was on the verge of being asked to leave after having "achieved" a 1.2 cumulative grade point average. But that's a topic for another book.

HIGH ANXIETY

Not counting asking girls out, I experienced my first "sales-call anxiety" in college. I needed more sales to pay for the higher college tuition, so I had to prospect for new business. After my last class of the day, I would run to my car, slap on a dress shirt and tie and call on nearby companies to sell printing. I remember feeling really anxious about selling.

Looking back, I can see that I feared rejection and felt needy when having to ask for business. The root cause of that uncomfortable feeling was a mystery to me. In high school, I was compelled to sell due to the fear of not being able to go to Aquinas. In college, I didn't feel as strongly about doing the academic work so the scales of my anxiety tipped from a "healthy" fear—not going to Aquinas—toward an unhealthy fear of rejection. As a result, I did not prospect nearly as much as necessary.

After my sudden exit from college, I went to work in my dad's printing company in a production capacity. I spent nine years working for my father before I decided to start my own company.

ENTER THE MENTOR

My dad deserves a sincere "thank you" for all he did for me. I had told him that eventually I wanted to be a company president, and he had the foresight to suggest I mentor under C.S. "Chic" Lewis. Chic was a management consultant, strict as a drill sergeant, but also a person who cared deeply. He saw me as a long shot at running my own company because I had flunked out of school. He gave me, in his words, an "MBA the hard way." I studied under him for those nine years.

I had a sound business idea—a whole new business concept, in fact—a good reputation in the printing industry and an insane work ethic, but no money. Even with my personal guarantee, putting up everything I owned as collateral, I found I could only cover a portion of what I needed to open the business. My dad stepped up and backed me by cosigning a loan for the additional $1,000,000 I needed. All this caused enormous pressure because I did not want to let anyone down—especially my father.

My plan was simple and, in hindsight, a bit naive. I was going to be the inside guy. I would oversee software development, enhance production and manage my people. Like many young entrepreneurs, I saw the sales department as a "black box" and had no idea how to run it effectively. I had a great product and service and thought all I needed was a couple of salespeople to sell for me. I hired two established sales representatives with plenty of industry experience and paid them both a large salary—a $90,000 package back in 1991! I didn't mind paying them well if they sold.

The only problem was that they didn't bring in sales. Before long, I was six months into the business and bleeding cash. My line of credit was running out. I was terrified of defaulting on my dad, as well as losing my house. I suffered from horrible stress under all this pressure.

"LOBSTER FOR TWO, PLEASE"

My breaking—and turning—point came when I was reviewing receipts. I saw that one of my salespeople had submitted a dinner check for an unusually large amount of money. I asked her what the receipt was for, and she responded that it was for a lobster dinner where she treated a prospect (who had ultimately said, "No, thanks," to her proposal). After I heard this, I walked back to my office, shut the door, turned off the lights and started to cry.

I knew then that my two "salespeople" were not going to sell anything. I didn't know what to do. I came to the conclusion that I had to fire them both, and I delayed this decision for several more weeks because I was personally terrified at the prospect of selling.

I fired them on a Friday, so I had a few days until I was forced to run the gauntlet of making sales calls myself. My strategy was pretty primitive. I would show up nervously at a prospect's office and ask for an opportunity to bid for a project. I was willing to stay until they gave me a chance or until they called the cops. I am not exaggerating. I was that desperate. Looking back, I'm sure that the prospects saw my fear and desperation and took advantage of this.

I called on prospects with the intention of making a presentation, asking for the order and then handling objections. As a result, I ended up chasing opportunities for months on end, trying to get them to close. It was exhausting, but better than the alternative of going broke.

My desire to succeed paid off. Within two years, I was selling a lot. I sold large deals and long-term contracts into numerous markets. However, I was still not comfortable selling. I sold big-name accounts while still suffering from sales-call anxiety. To help alleviate my pain, I went to every sales seminar that I could find: Zig Ziglar, Tom Hopkins, Tony Robbins and many others. All of them were inspirational and great speakers. Nevertheless, within a couple weeks the inspiration wore off and I was back to my usual stressed-out self, still fighting the fear of making sales calls.

Our advanced production processes were very disruptive to the marketplace, and we were beating the competition soundly by being the low-cost provider. As a result, many older established competitors ended up closing, giving us even more market share. But in spite of all we had going for us, I still had not reached the level of having a professional salesperson. Why? Because no one can sell as well as the company president. When owners sell for their own companies, they carry the intangible advantage of having the final say, and buyers take comfort from this. Owners also possess an unmatched belief in their company. When the buyer is dealing with the top of the organization, not the salesperson, the dynamic changes.

I see similar situations with a lot of companies that seek out training in the Sandler sales principles. The owner can sell with little resistance, but the new sales hires cannot. The owners are frustrated and angry because their salespeople can't close deals as well as they can. The reality is that the salespeople will never be on par with the owner. Any sales strategy has to allow for this fact. The owner's ability is typically not transferrable.

TIME TO CASH OUT?

From the start, I built my company with the intention of selling it. After seven years in business we had facilities in three states, and our client list was a "Who's Who" of top companies in the mid-1990s: Mattel, Bausch and Lomb, Fisher-Price, Marvel Entertainment, Sara Lee and Kodak. Our company led our industry segment in profitability for the final six years that I owned it, and, as a result, the company was admitted into the industry's Hall of Fame in 2000.

Like many entrepreneurs, my plan from the start was to cash out and walk away from the company. Unfortunately, when I put the company up for sale, I learned a hard lesson: I had nothing any intelligent investor would want to buy. As potential suitors looked at the company, they soon realized that I was the number one sales-person. Who in their right mind would buy that company? When I left, so would the sales. I had fallen into the trap where so many entrepreneurs find themselves stuck: I couldn't sell my company because I didn't build a sales team that could succeed without me.

After getting no serious offers, I realized that to reach my goal of selling the company, I had to build a functional sales team that was not dependent on me. I still carried the scars from the two non-producing salespeople who had cost me a ton of money. If my new effort were to succeed, I would have to become a sales leader as opposed to being the sales producer. Seeing that I needed help, Chic stepped in once again to advise me. I built a strong sales team in two years and went back to market. With a self-sufficient sales force that was producing the vast majority of our revenue, I sold the company for a sizeable sum of money.

THE SANDLER CONNECTION

Up to this point in my career, I had yet to hear of David Sandler. It would take a national tragedy for me to make that particular transition.

After I sold my company, Dad asked me to come back to his firm and assume the presidency in order to help him sell it. Against the advice of Chic and my wife, I decided to take the position. The mission was to grow sales another $20 million and then put the company on the market. At the time, that was a realistic expecta-tion given the massive industry consolidation then occurring.

When I became president, I intended my focus to be on operations. I did not want to get involved in sales because I still hated sales. I loved finance and production. I was going to depend on the current sales manager to handle the sales team while I focused on the rest of the business.

Then history threw me a curve. Nine months into my new job, the country was devastated by the terrorist attacks of September 11, 2001. As everyone knows, the business community was hit hard. However, our company felt the pinch more than most printers because the majority of our work was centered on retail and consumer spending all but stopped. To make matters worse, our company was heavily leveraged due to debt taken on for an expansion, which resulted in defaulting on our loan covenants.

The impact on the company from the events of September 11 forced me back into sales again. About this time, I was introduced to Sandler. I hired a local Sandler trainer to work with our team, and I sat in on the sessions to make sure that the training was up to par.

"THE BIGGEST COMEBACK SINCE LAZARUS"

I found the Sandler content to be great. I studied it extensively. Soon I was using the Sandler principles to help guide the closing of multi-million dollar contracts, many of which the company still enjoys today. I didn't do this on my own. We had a great sales leader (Jim Monte) and a handful of salespeople who embraced Sandler's concepts and worked hard to turn things around.

We won contracts in an intensely competitive environment where we were the highest-priced bidder. I remember the year-end conference with the president of the bank, who was probably planning to recall our credit right after the meeting. He looked at our year-end financials and said, "You guys made the biggest comeback since Lazarus!"

SELLER'S REMORSE

Sales were on track again, so it became time to put the company on the market. Once this process started, my father and other top stakeholders began showing seller's remorse. When I had come into the job, we had agreed that I was going to make the majority of my money on the sale of the company, and now I did not see that happening. Rather than stay on, I decided to give the board a year's notice and go back to school to earn an MBA.

After graduating with my MBA, I went looking for my next venture. I wanted to purchase a company or enter into a series of smaller investments with several companies. To make this plan work, I needed to increase my exposure to other businesses outside of my network. I decided to open a Sandler Training Center. Austin, Texas, was on the list of available territories. Even though I had never even visited the city, I chose Austin as a long overdue favor to my wife Linda, who wanted out of the cold upstate New York weather. As we were moving to Texas, I recall thinking, *What could be simpler than a business selling sales training?* As I had a successful background selling multi-million dollar deals, I thought that selling sales training would be a cakewalk.

I wish! Take away my network, my financial motivation (because I had enough money to retire), my industry reputation and my title, and what did I have left? Just my hidden unresolved self-limiting beliefs. What were they? Fear of rejection, cold-call anxiety and the need for approval, to name a few. Unlike any other time in my career, I had to cold call at a staggering rate. To make it more difficult, I was selling something intangible, a service that people did not understand or want, regardless of how much they needed it. Now I had to sell for real.

I had to come to grips with the stark reality that I needed to change, but I thought that I could fake it by spending a fortune on advertising. That didn't work. I got no leads. That's when I realized that I had to sell again.

NO WAY TO FAKE IT

The Sandler network is filled with the best, most disciplined salespeople that I have ever known. While I watched them work, I quickly learned I could not make it by faking it. They could sniff out a phony. Mostly through initial peer pressure, I had no choice but to let go of what had made me successful in the past and face my self-limiting beliefs head on. I had come to the realization that what had worked for me in the past would not work for me now.

The Sandler network has an overriding value: "Be a product of the product." If I were to accomplish that, I had to deal with my high need for approval and tendency to become emotionally involved during the sales process. Most of all, I had to change the sales call from a meeting about myself and my company to an interview centered solely on prospects and their needs. These changes were a tremendous challenge for me. I had to rely heavily on my Sandler coach, Tom Fecteau, whom I met with weekly for many years. I went to a psychologist regularly for several years and used journaling to help monitor my self-talk. Most importantly, I had my patient wife who was forced to withstand my constant requests to "hear me out."

In closing, let me share with you something more personal: While my family life looked normal from the outside, it wasn't. That was the case up until I started with Sandler. Sure, we attended church every week. I coached and watched the kids' sporting events, and I was out in the social scene with Linda on a regular basis. In reality the combination of my poor communication skills and my relentless pursuit for perfection in business and education damaged the family to the point where Linda and I agreed to a separation.

The situation did not look promising. I was expecting the worst outcome. Over time, though, things started to change. Resources like the Extended DISC assessment and Sandler's other principles enabled me to improve my communication skills. Within a year after starting Sandler, I had begun the process of rebuilding the relationships with my family.

Ten years later, our family is stronger than it's ever been. Talk about a breakthrough! In the end, the greatest gift that Sandler gave me was helping me get my family back together. That's been the best deal I ever closed.

CHAPTER TWO

The Accidental Salesperson

ADAM BOYD

I didn't intend to go into sales. I got here by accident.

I started my working life teaching high school English and coaching football. I'd graduated with a degree in literature. I didn't know what to do with that, but I did know I wanted to coach football. So that's what I did.

My path quickly took a different turn after just one year. I watched other coaches around me struggling with the same time commitments that I was. Our 100-hour work weeks left little time for family, and the money wasn't ever going to be great. I wanted a

> *"Only by risking failure can we accomplish anything."* —David Sandler

family someday—and I wanted to spend time with them—so I left coaching and teaching. For the next few years I bounced around: tended bar, waited tables, delivered party supplies, managed a website and scanned books. I wasn't sure where I was going.

I didn't intend to go to business school either. At 26, I knew a few things: I wanted to live in Austin, Texas; I never wanted work to dictate my location or schedule; and I wanted to learn how to make money. So I chose to attend the Acton School of Business in Austin. They made three promises: I'd learn how to learn, make money, and live a life of meaning. All three of these promises spoke to me. I never applied to anywhere else. It was Acton or nothing.

WHAT'S NEXT?

During business school, the faculty and staff pushed me and my fellow students to discover what we wanted to do next in our lives. I still had no clue. I was underwater with the workload, trying to build sound financial models, understand business operations and keep up with my peers. I was sleeping five hours a night, so I felt I could punt on the job issue. All I really knew was that I wanted to make money and decide where I lived, not have that determined for me by some large employer. I was open to what that would look like.

I took stock of the talent around me in business school and where people were headed professionally: operations; finance; marketing; and product management. No one was looking at sales. I saw an opportunity.

What's more, I perked up when Karl Scheible, the co-author of this book and our company's president, came to speak to us about sales. I didn't know much about him other than he'd run a company or two, and worked with businesses on growing sales. When he offered to have us come visit him after graduation, I took him up on it.

OPENING THE BLACK BOX

Unbeknownst to Karl, I hoped to work under him while I figured out my career path, which I was certain involved owning and running a company someday. Since all the people I knew were avoiding sales, I decided I'd learn it. My classmates—and thousands of business owners and CEOs—tend to throw sales into some black box and assume someone else will do it for them if they pay them enough.

Karl evaluated me with some specific assessments, read the findings and said, "Kid, you're not going to make it in sales. Why do you want to do this?" (Looking back, I think he may have been testing me.)

I told him I wanted to run a company and that I needed to be able to sell to do so.

"This will be tougher for you than becoming a lawyer or doctor," he told me.

I didn't believe him and insisted he take me on as a project. He gave me a shot.

My gig? To make cold calls to fill events where Karl was speaking. Every day I'd sit in a windowless room and call on business owners and CEOs from a book of lists. Karl was merciful enough to pay me $15/hour, plus $100 for every person I put into one of the events, as he knew he was likely to close a good portion of the attendees. Simple enough, right?

I took the job because I wanted to learn sales. I have a knack for involving myself in efforts above my pay grade. I didn't realize how ego-deflating and draining this process would be.

It was brutal. I dreaded going to the office each day and facing that phone. In cold calling, especially when you're starting out, you deal with a lot of *noes*. Hundreds of them. Eventually thousands. To me, those *noes* often felt like rejection, even failure.

All my life, I'd done well at most things I'd attempted when a score was being kept. School had grades, and football had points. There were winners and losers. I was largely accustomed to winning, especially if I put in enough effort. Here, the effort and the results didn't show any quick correlation.

By some miracle I booked two people for the first event we held. That was the hardest $200 I ever earned—and the best. But I had three no-shows.

Still I found myself failing daily, call after call. The overwhelming feeling of failure didn't fade. I'd make 40–50 calls a day. Some days I tried to avoid dialing by researching companies and their executives. I told myself this was "self-development" work. I wanted to get to the day's end as quickly as possible.

It wasn't that anything terrible happened. No one yelled at me. I didn't get fired, and I was earning enough money to feed myself. What was so painful was how I felt.

- I felt like a failure because I wasn't getting any traction; I saw no measurable improvement for a long time, nor any increase in earnings.
- I felt stupid because I didn't know what to say on calls.
- I felt scared because I didn't know if I could make it.
- I felt upset because my business-school classmates appeared wildly successful while I languished by the phone.
- I felt frustrated that it seemed so difficult to succeed in my professional life, a feeling I'd battled since I left coaching six years earlier.
- I felt tired of being broke.

"PLEASE DON'T PICK UP"

As a result of these negative feelings, picking up the phone created huge anxiety for me. I felt nauseated thinking about it. My heart raced after I dialed and listened to the phone ringing. I'd sometimes say to myself, "Please don't pick up, please don't pick up," because I wanted to win some sort of credit for simply dialing the phone. However, even if I didn't reach decision makers, I had to talk with secretaries and assistants or leave messages on voicemail, trying to generate something—a callback, a spark of interest, anything. I felt so small and inadequate.

Fridays were the best because I didn't have to be in the office the following two days. It wasn't that being in the office was so bad—it's that I was so was bad in the office. I had yet to develop any consistent skill or success at what I was doing. Weekends provided a guilt-free license to stay as far away from the phone as I wanted. Sunday evenings were the worst, though, because I knew that when the next morning arrived, I faced another five days of doing something that appeared to have no happy ending in sight, no turning point when my results would hockey-stick upward with success, sales, money, fame and *Fortune* magazine.

That was year one. Years two and three saw me work like mad to build a small book of business, almost exclusively off referrals and networking. I employed Sandler's three-foot rule: Talk to anyone you can reach out and touch about what they do and what you do. This led to conversations that led to sales. One of my first meaningful experiences using this method came in a Goodwill store with an eventual client who led me to at least five other pieces of business.

I went to every networking event I could find and seized any chance I could to meet people: chamber of commerce events; meetups; happy hours of every sort; groups ranging from bankers to Harley riders; speed networking; charity functions. You name it, I attended. I left with business cards and was always drained because I am naturally more introverted than I appear. My efforts paid off. I culled those cards, called on those people and developed more business.

COLD CALL BLUES

However, even when I got these "wins," I didn't count them because either Karl closed some of them or they were outside the realm I'd been tasked to learn: the phone.

I still cold called and still posted goose eggs in turning the calls into business. The nerves were still there each time I made a call, but I was getting used to them. They weren't the big issue anymore. Instead, I had moved to higher level angst: struggling to ask hard questions, to say tough things, to push back, to ask for more money or bigger commitments.

I also had a hard time "staying in the moment" and listening to prospects because of head trash. I was convinced I wouldn't get the business. While they were talking, I was worrying about what to say or ask next; I couldn't fully engage. I muddled along.

Why did I stick around so long? I'm stubborn. If I begin something, especially any activity where others can see my results, I'm driven to keep at it until I reach some level of satisfactory competence. I hate quitting, but what I most hate is being terrible when I quit.

THE SHIFT

Around the third year, things started to change in both my personal and professional lives. The former had a major impact on the latter. First, my wife got pregnant. I realized I would soon have two dependents. I couldn't afford to be afraid of asking prospects tough questions anymore. Soon there would be a little boy counting on me to do the difficult things in life, like pick up a phone and ask a stranger for a conversation.

I noticed a real shift while talking to an entrepreneur who'd been referred to me. He was a small business owner who'd lost 70% of his business in the prior year. I saw he was hurting, and I asked, "Well, would you want to get together to see if I can help?" He said, "No, I don't think so." Above my desk hung a photo of my little boy-to-be's sonogram. It reminded me that he needed me to get the job done. I looked at that sonogram and mustered enough guts to ask, "Are you sure? You've lost 70% of your business in the last year, and you don't want to see if I can help?" His response? "Sure. Let's do that."

The shift continued when my son was born. I'd lost 70% of my own business in the month prior to his birth. Some clients' agreements were up. Others decided they'd try to have their sales manager do my job. Some were cutting costs. It hit all at once. When my son Kaufman (named for my high school football coach) arrived, I was overjoyed, but also terrified. My wife had stopped working so she could take care of him, as we'd agreed she would, and I feared I'd let them down and we'd all starve. I had to change.

Contracts were a rarity in our office at that time. They were reserved for only very large deals, which I wasn't doing. However, now I had to create a predictable monthly income, as two people were depending on me. So I began asking for contracts.

PURPOSE

Previously, clients paid us month-to-month because we thought contracts weren't enforceable in our line of work. That was the excuse I made. The result was that we expected clients to stay for a long time, although they might leave after a few months if they had some success and thought they'd "gotten it figured out." Now, I was more afraid of not having secured commitments from customers than I was of asking for those commitments. Kaufman had given me a purpose that trumped my fear.

In the next year, my fourth with Karl, business started closing more regularly. I didn't set the world on fire, but I kept improving. I still made many mistakes, and I probably left a lot of money on the table, but my attitude was more positive. My sales reflected this.

I saw an uptick in the amount and size of business I was closing. Deals came more easily, and I started to receive more high-quality introductions and referrals. Accounts grew in size, and I landed a number of speaking events.

CHANGING TARGETS

Prior to this, I rarely met with large company owners. Even when I did, I felt in my heart of hearts I didn't belong there. This had to change. Many of my early clients were individual salespeople or solo entrepreneurs (two groups I still enjoy), but there was more money in larger companies. I had to shift my thinking to begin closing them.

I grew up in the South, where you defer to your elders and use, "No, sir," and "Yes, sir," with those in authority. Mentally and emotionally, that mindset prevented me from seeing myself as a CEO's peer, since many of these people were two or three decades older than I was. Through journaling, I wrote out my fears, worries and doubts. I began to see that they weren't true, and that they were holding me back. Not only was I a CEO's peer, but in the area of sales and sales management, I was the expert. I realized these people should be paying me well for my advice. And that's what happened.

I began asking prospects tougher questions because those were the questions they needed to hear. Questions like: "What happens if you don't change? Can you live with the status quo?" People opened up more. Before, my need for approval and deference to those who were older prevented me from asking these questions. Now, I felt better about myself because I asked them.

"LET'S TALK ABOUT MONEY"

What's more, I spoke more frankly about money. I remember, growing up, how my parents told me, "You don't ask what things cost." Specifically, I remember my father and late grandfather telling me this on my seventh birthday when I asked about the cost of a gift. I have no clue why I asked that, but I left with no doubt about the impropriety of my transgression.

Sitting in front of presidents and CEOs, I had to learn to ask what it cost them to live with their problems. That was tough. I also had to ask how much they were willing to pay me to solve the problem. That was harder. I began journaling daily, "I easily talk about money." By "daily," I mean every single day, five days per week, 50 weeks per year. I worked on this belief going into sales calls. Over time, after many failures, I saw some change in my interaction with prospects. We discussed money.

Between my fourth and fifth year, I went deeper and wider with my use of a journal. Sandler teaches sales representatives and managers to keep a journal of attitudes and behaviors because the work is so emotional and the highs and lows wear on so many people. I worked on affirmations in my journal every day, like so many other people do. But I added a component I learned from a client: I worked diligently on visualizing success, both near-term and long-term. I began thinking about areas of my life and what it would look and feel like to have the success of my dreams. I'd spend up to 45 minutes some days working in my journal, rewriting negative beliefs and imagining how it felt to succeed and grow in the ways I desired.

As a result, my fifth year in the business I reached new levels of personal sales production. I even began receiving some awards and recognition for how much I was selling. Interestingly, I was making the amount of money that I had written about in my journal two years prior—it just took two years of imagining it to see it happen.

ANATOMY OF A BREAKTHROUGH

Yes, I was making money. It allowed my wife and me to pay off some student loans, to replace old cars, to build a house, even to save and invest. I saw clients making their own breakthroughs and reach their own record levels of production. Many felt better about themselves because of the demons they had slain. I felt better about myself, too. I was enjoying my work. No longer did fear dominate my Sunday nights. I had a positive expectation for the week.

What led to my change? A few things. First, I realized I had to get serious when I saw the sonogram. Not too many months later, there was Kaufman in my arms! Talk about motivation. Suddenly I was willing to do the work I didn't always want to do—more networking, asking for more introductions and finding organizations that would bring in speakers. These all entailed the risk of rejection and feelings of failure. But my son was screaming every night at three in the morning. He wasn't worried whether or not I made friends or was comfortable—he just wanted to eat.

Second, I began to clarify my goals. I visualized what I really wanted in my life and saw myself having that success. It wasn't easy at first, seeing myself close large deals or even one large deal a week. But I kept a journal. I wrote about my "successes"—both current and future—each day.

Writing enabled me to think about how deals would close, what they'd look like, and how I'd feel in those sales calls. I also thought about how much money I'd make each month. I looked at my vision boards containing images of how I wanted to feel and what I wanted to achieve.

IMAGINATION TRUMPS THINKING

Earlier in my career, I'd try thinking my way through problems. As I confronted more challenges, I realized my imagination was more important in some ways than my ability to solve problems. That's because imagination activates feelings. Those emotions either enabled me to employ Sandler's techniques and behave as I needed to or kept me hiding in fear.

Changing deeply-held beliefs about myself wasn't easy. A typical day of journaling involved 30–40 minutes of affirmations and visualization to reprogram my head trash—my limiting beliefs about myself and the world around me. Of course, that was in addition to all the work anyone who wants to succeed in sales must do: prospecting, networking and serving customers.

IT'S NOT ABOUT "GETTING THERE"

Success, I realized, involved seeking out opportunities to succeed while knowing I might fail. There was a lesson there, too. Eventually I learned to see failure as a teaching tool, something that grew and strengthened my role as a seller. It had no impact on my identity or who I am as a person.

I have left behind much of the insecurity and fear I possessed when I graduated from business school. I am still happily married with two children (Louisa having joined us in late 2013). I'm blessed to have plenty of time to spend with them while I earn a good living. I've even returned to coaching football 40 hours per week each fall!

I see my hopes unfolding before me. Best of all, I am helping others visualize and pursue their own dreams.

I've learned from Sandler that success is not about getting "there." It's about the person we are becoming along the way. That's what sales and Sandler have given me: the attitudes, behaviors and techniques to grow—and keep on growing.

PART TWO

The Overachievers

We've trained countless sales professionals over the years. Everyone in our classes who had a deep desire to grow in the profession and wanted help making more money or working the sales process with less stress improved. Period. No exceptions.

Yet looking back at all the people we've trained, we can't help noticing an elite group of people whose stories stand out because they overachieved during their training with us. Many of these people had the deck stacked against them in some way.

We would like everyone in every program to overachieve, so we started taking a closer look at this specific group of people. A clear pattern started to emerge. They all had major issues with some internal script or belief that was limiting their success.

However, their high desire and commitment to improving their career led them to attempt the Sandler behaviors in spite of their fears. When comparing our findings to the observations of other Sandler trainers throughout the network, their findings were similar to ours. This is the profile of the overachiever.

The people that we chose for this part of the book carry many different job titles—salespeople, sales managers, presidents and CEOs—but they are all overachievers whose breakthroughs we had the honor of observing firsthand. They had something else in common: None of them are what anyone would consider to be a natural-born salesperson!

CHAPTER 3

Learning to Say "No"

DUSTIN WELLS, CEO
HEADSPRING SYSTEMS

W e first met Dustin Wells in 2007. He resembled (and still does) the typical under-40 Austin entrepreneur—jeans, a loud and loose shirt and flip-flops. Like many young people drawn to Austin, he came here for the music. He actually played in one of the top local bands in his 20s. When we met, he came across as quiet and introspective. Through all of his success over the years, he has remained humble. His posture and expressions have always hinted at a subtle sense of humor.

> "Sales is not a place for getting your
> needs met." —David Sandler

Shortly after starting a family, Dustin realized he needed a gig that could pay the mortgage and leave some extra money for diapers. For better or worse, the Austin music scene wasn't doing that. Dustin took a job as a loan processor in a mortgage company, where he soon identified costly inefficiencies in the operations.

PROBLEM SOLVER

A problem solver by nature, Dustin took it upon himself to study basic computer programming because he knew software could automate several manual tasks at work. He learned basic coding and built a new system for the company. He told us, later on, that this experience gave him a mission: using technology to make business more efficient.

Dustin's first try at starting his own business sprang from his desire to look out for his son, who was in daycare. He opened a company that installed video systems in childcare centers so parents could see their children during the day. He made a sale early on, but then sold only one more system over the next two years. He folded up shop and decided to try his hand at consulting.

Slowly but steadily, he found work. After first year billings of $18,000, business doubled almost every year until he was doing several hundred thousand dollars annually by 2007. That was when Dustin and I met.

THE MAN WHO COULDN'T SAY "NO"

Asked why he wanted sales training, Dustin gave several good reasons. He said, "My sales are too difficult to forecast. I can manage most aspects of the business pretty easily, but the sales part is too sporadic. I need to find a way to get sales beyond word of mouth and friends of friends. What if that business goes away? Sales are the lifeblood of this company. If I can't make sales come through the door, I'm in trouble. I have a process for everything, but not sales."

In our firm, we always assess someone before we train them. Dustin's assessment looked terrible. He had a very high need for approval back then, something he readily admits today. In other words, he did not want to rock the boat with prospects because he might upset them and they wouldn't like him. This limited his willingness and ability to prospect, ask tough questions, go after business and essentially run any sort of sales process effectively. He was too afraid of rejection.

Dustin couldn't say, "No," and he never wanted to hear, "No."

LEADING BY EXAMPLE

Dustin also hated to talk about money. It made him anxious. As a result, he avoided any budget conversations. In many cases, he would spend hours designing a $75,000 solution, only to learn after the presentation that the potential client only had a $7,500 budget. That kind of rude awakening would sometimes happen after multiple meetings with a prospect. The Sandler Selling System methodology teaches salespeople to go for the *no* first, and that someone learns to get to *yes* only after they've gotten enough *noes*.

Dustin's aversion to discussing money presented a real problem. Sandler requires sellers to have candid conversations about money early in the qualification process. Otherwise, a salesperson may spend a lot of valuable time and energy with a prospect who doesn't have the money or is unwilling to spend it. We asked ourselves, "How on Earth can this guy possibly get through the training, much less apply it?"

We told Dustin that it was OK if he hired a salesperson. To be honest, we encouraged that route because we knew the change required for him to succeed in sales would be both significant and difficult.

Dustin dug in his heels. "If I'm going to build a strong company, I need to be able to lead by example." He signed up to train with us.

We wondered. Could this guy really make it? Could he pull it off? We didn't see how.

Dustin later told us that he was thinking, "Who the heck are these guys to tell me that I have a need for approval?"

Fortunately for all of us, he did have a need for approval or he would have kicked us out of his office right then and there! In talking to Dustin about this book, we asked him if he ever identified the root of his high need for approval.

"Yes," he said. "It goes back to childhood. I grew up in a divorced home with stepparents and stepsiblings, so things were always a little chaotic with switching between my parents' homes week to week. My strategy was to fit in and not rock the boat. I avoided any conflict and wanted to stay out of the way as much as possible. The result? I didn't learn to interact with authority figures in any sort of healthy way. As an adult, I couldn't see myself as their peer."

He went on, "Interestingly enough, though, this experience as a child taught me to handle multiple challenges at once and to really focus. I learned to tune other things out, no matter how distracting or upsetting."

THE TURNING POINT

Nine months into Dustin's training, we announced a "Live Cold-Call Boot Camp" to all of our clients. In these, our trainers make live cold calls on a speakerphone in front of an audience. It's sales training on a high wire without a net. Dustin, one of our students, asked if he could make some calls during the training session. That had never happened before and hasn't happened since. We thought to ourselves, "This guy is out of his mind." But despite his fears, he did it!

Need for approval and the fear of rejection keep most people from doing the work of looking for new business. For those like Dustin who are stubborn enough to push through those feelings, the struggle is personal. We can still see Dustin sweating in his suit and tie, his hands shaking as he picked up the phone. Nevertheless, a few calls into his session, Dustin made a connection—and proceeded to book an appointment for a very large opportunity.

We later asked Dustin why he had done this. "I needed a deadline. I knew I needed some impending event to force me to do it, to prepare myself to hear, 'No,' and move on. I couldn't walk in there in front of my peers and not do well. This is what pushed me to practice. That helped me so much, putting myself out there. I was sick getting started, but I survived."

It was this same tenacity, this same unwillingness to quit, that allowed Dustin to push through his issues discussing money. In our time working together, his average sale increased from $40,000 to $350,000. He said, "One of the highlights was using the Sandler principles to close my first seven-figure deal!"

FAST COMPANY

How is Dustin's company doing today? As this book goes to press, the current sales target is $20 million—and he's on track to hit it. This growth rate has landed Headspring Systems on the INC 500 list and the *Austin Business Journal*'s "Fast 50" list numerous times.

We asked Dustin, "How did you overcome the enormous internal issues that were holding you back?" His response was a keeper: "Aside from learning and following the Sandler system, I spent a lot of time working on my self-limiting beliefs and assumptions. For instance, I used to think that if I called prospects, I was bothering them. I rewrote that belief so that I told myself, 'There are people who need my help. I should call them to see if they need me.'"

Like a lot of Sandler disciples, Dustin used a journal daily to "rescript" beliefs that were counter-productive. David Sandler taught that the use of a journal could show someone how unproductive old beliefs can be. The journaling process usually leads to a breakthrough realization: The things that gave us success in the past may not help get us where we want to go next.

Prior to 2007, Dustin's selling process consisted of presenting prospects with a blizzard of options. He focused on all the technical aspects of his service and solution, and there were lots from which to choose. He didn't ask for any commitments, assuming people would buy if they wanted to work with him. While this was a traditional and seemingly straightforward approach, it led to frustratingly unpredictable results. He produced a large number of time-consuming proposals but endured a very low close rate.

He spent time generating proposals rather than selling for three reasons. First, it was all he knew, having never been trained to sell. Second, it fed his need for approval and the desire to have someone tell him how smart he was, which he heard often. Third, he was uncomfortable asking for business because, in his opinion, that might make someone else uncomfortable.

Today his company does far fewer proposals—only one or two each year. Instead, they now have a formal sales process that leads to a much higher close rate. Not surprisingly, Dustin continues to send his new hires to Sandler for training.

AN ATTITUDE REVOLUTION

When he started out, Dustin did not see himself as a leader or entrepreneur. Now he does, and rightly so. He has come to realize that he is the only thing ever standing in his way. To address this, he does something outside of his comfort zone daily. For example, he might say something out loud that he might not normally say due to his need for approval or to avoid conflict.

Was all of his success due to sales training? Not all of it. It was supported by his willingness to do the necessary behaviors to change the way he thought and ultimately sold. Most importantly, Dustin worked diligently on the "Attitude" point of Sandler's Behavior/Attitude/Technique (BAT) triangle. He disregarded his assumptions about prospects. Real change takes time, but he was committed to doing the work—day after day, month after month, year after year. He continued to question his beliefs and assumptions when they didn't lead him to the result he desired. This was not a one-year transformation. Dustin continues to work on his non-productive scripts and beliefs today, seven years later.

Someone really smart once said that the mind is a pain to stretch and grow, but once you stretch it, it never goes back. Or words to that effect. It sounds like a good song lyric. Maybe Dustin will record it one day.

CHAPTER 4

The Entrepreneurial Breakthrough

MARIO FEGHALI, CEO
SPAREFOOT

O ut of the many thousands of salespeople we have trained in the Sandler methodology, the most typical learning path we see starts with an eager representative who is captivated by the Sandler concepts. Then when it's actually time to try the concepts in the field—on real prospects—salespeople often run into an invisible wall: the internal confrontation between comfortable old beliefs and the non-traditional new ideas they have been

> "The only way to fail at prospecting is to
> fail to prospect." —David Sandler

taught. Unless they are highly motivated and have the discipline to push through the hard times, meaningful change won't happen.

Mario Feghali was the opposite of the typical student. He started selling in a way that conflicted with his own natural beliefs. By chance, the Sandler principles were completely in line with Mario's internal thinking. Change came easier for Mario than it did for most, due to this natural fit and his own aggressive learning style. Rarely do we see students as engaged as Mario was in class. He didn't just take in the concepts; he devoured them.

THE ROAD TRIP

Mario was into his third year of pre-med, getting ready to take the MCATs, when he found himself driving to his mother's house in Bakersfield, California. His car was stuffed to the max with the possessions of the friend with him, Chuck. Mario had talked his mother into agreeing to store all of Chuck's worldly belongings while Chuck was out of the country.

As Mario and Chuck talked during the drive, they wondered aloud if there was an easier way to find inexpensive storage closer to home. Their talk evolved into the idea of creating a simple website that facilitated peer-to-peer storage. They figured that there were plenty of people who would be more than eager to rent out extra space in their house for a reasonable rate. Chuck was living proof that there are likewise plenty of people who could use cheap storage. The idea made sense economically and practically. Had Chuck used a commercial storage facility instead of Mario's mother's home, he would have spent a couple of thousand dollars while he was away.

AN IDEA WITH LEGS

I asked Mario to explain how he and Chuck went about launching SpareFoot, which has grown from 3 to 190 employees in the six years we have worked with him. Mario explained, "The first thing that we did was write a business plan in 2008 to help raise money. Looking back, I am amazed at how much I had to invent to complete the initial 60-page plan. I had no idea what I was doing; I made things up as I went along. Soon I found myself begging for $5,000 to $10,000 from friends, family and strangers. This was tough on me because I have barely seen more than $200 before. We somehow managed to raise $60,000 and were ready to start.

"The initial plan was a bit flawed. We had plenty of people signing up on the website who needed space, but not many were signing up to rent their space. I started to imagine nightmare scenarios where people with less than honorable intentions were looking to stash illegal content on an unsuspecting landlord's property. I could see the headline: 'Grandmother busted for storing drugs.'

"In 2009 we were starting to attract a good amount of PR after being written up in a local publication. Then we noticed something interesting. Storage facilities were starting to sign up on our site. I had no idea why, so I called them to find out. They saw our user base as a target market to rent their storage space. That's when we made a major change to our strategy. We began to see ourselves as the engine that matched the consumer with local storage facilities. I envisioned our website as the Expedia or Priceline of the storage industry.

"This idea had legs, but we knew we needed more money and expertise. We applied to a business incubator for help. This was a complex and tedious process, and we were turned down twice. Finally, on our third attempt, the Capital Factory in Austin, Texas, accepted us."

"THERE WAS NOTHING FOR SALES"

"The incubator program was a huge help," Mario continued, "but I soon discovered they did not have any sales expertise. We had access to product development, marketing, operations and investors, but there was nothing for sales. I thought to myself that this was going to be a problem because I needed to cold call storage companies and talk them into signing up with us.

"Up until then, my only sales experience was working for my uncle's Little Caesar's Pizza franchise. My uncle told me to up-sell every customer who called in, so as to increase orders of cheesy bread or wings. He explained that the margin is higher on those items so I had to keep moving them. I was only 12 or 13 at the time—but I got the message, and I up-sold the customers!

"Looking back on those early days at the incubator, I realize now that I was boxed into a corner. For the business to succeed, I had get storage facilities to sign up fast. I was able to sell some of the larger companies who had multiple locations early on, but there were nearly 4,000 mom-and-pop single location facilities. That was a ton of calling.

"Based on my experience with sales as a kid, the societal sales stereotypes and how people had been sold to all my life, I figured that all I needed to do was act enthusiastic and pushy and I would be successful. So I worked to adopt this style. I learned to talk louder and faster, and I adopted a higher pitch, which was the opposite of my natural deeper voice and measured rate of speaking. I tried to convince people by presenting all of our features up front. I did all the talking. I never considered asking a question or listening to the customer. And I was being rejected consistently. No one cared about what I had to say. I began to hate making the calls. My internal dialogue was horrible. Inside, I was saying things like: 'I can't do this. I'm no good at making these calls.'

"Out of pure desperation, I reached out to my brother who was a successful salesperson for Frito-Lay. I ran my pitch by him and will never forget his response—he told me that I sounded like crap. I asked for help, but he didn't have any better ideas! There is a difference between selling snacks and storage, I guess."

THE MENTOR STEPS IN

Mario continued the story. "Shortly thereafter, I was checking in with Michael, my mentor at the Capital Factory. He asked me how things were going. I told him, 'Not good at all. I can't get people to talk to me.' He asked me to role-play my sales call. I agreed. He stopped me halfway through. He couldn't stand to hear more.

"Just like my brother had, Michael said that I sounded like crap. Then he asked me to describe to him what the typical old-fashioned salesperson sounds like. As I answered him, I realized that I was describing myself. On the call I was phony, fast-talking and self-centered. Forget the 30-second commercial. I had a 15-minute commercial!

"Michael was trained in Sandler. He gave me a few tips that provided immediate benefits. He taught me about the pattern interrupt—the art of not sounding like a salesperson. He told me that would buy me the few extra moments I needed to work on getting the prospect's attention. Michael also taught me that it's OK to get a *no*. I learned later that David Sandler said, 'You learn to get a *yes* by learning to get a *no* first.'

"Michael told me I needed to meet a guy named Karl Scheible. He invited Karl into the Capital Factory to teach an introductory sales class. When I heard Karl talk about the conflicting agendas of buyers and sellers, I started to get excited. Almost immediately, I could see what I was doing wrong. To my great relief, I discovered that to be effective at following Sandler, the first and most important step was to act naturally and be myself. Another breakthrough was the concept of setting the parameters for a meeting, especially the outcome, at the beginning of the meeting. In Sandler terms, this is called the Up-Front Contract. It helped me to establish equal business stature with my prospect. That gave me a sense of security, as I was a young guy with a new idea trying to sell to adults who were not immediately open to change."

THE TURNAROUND

"Things turned around for me almost immediately," Mario told us. "Raising money was easier. I was closing bigger deals and learning to handle the *no* much better. When I was shut down, I would relax, pause and respond with a Sandler basic: 'Before I hang up, can I ask you a quick question? Is my offering too complex or too expensive?' This got their attention. I got more conversations as a result. It was as simple as being brave ten seconds at a time. I decided to enroll in all the Sandler classes. I attended the President's Club and the Sandler Sales Leadership courses. I knew that I needed to be the best, so I started to work at it.

"I was OK until I closed all the available big deals—all the elephants. All that was left were the small companies, and it was not economical for me, the president of the company, to make outbound calls to small facilities. That left me in a strange and unfamiliar position: I needed salespeople.

"I tried everything I could think of to avoid building a sales staff. Frankly, I was afraid to hire salespeople. Eventually, though, it became clear that I could not close deals online. I tried outsourcing the sales function for a while. Those outsourced teams performed all right, but not great. Finally, out of options, I decided to hire my first sales representatives.

"My main goal was to start a team that didn't have the bad habits of a traditional salesperson. I wanted to build the best-in-class outbound sales team. I decided to train all the new hires in Sandler, to set expectations early and to hold them accountable. I saw the training—both in-house and at Sandler—as a resource, not an expense. The development and investment became part of our culture. I envisioned our employees as being the envy of the industry. I expect that if our salespeople decided for some reason to move on, they would be seen as 'badass' and a must-hire. They must be good to make it at SpareFoot."

NO AMBIGUITY

We asked Mario how he built a team that was so strong. He said, "There is no ambiguity when we hire someone. People know what it will take to become successful here and what will get them terminated. We clearly set the standards, and they understand that they will get warnings if they are off the mark. In fact, when people are dismissed, there are typically no hard feelings or drama. The parting is amicable, and the employees often apologize for letting us down.

"That's the ultimate result of keeping the employees' role separate from their identity. They don't take failing personally and, as a result, there is no reason not to let people go if they are not a good fit. The process is humane for both parties. The Sandler principles of transparency and managing expectations also play a role in my relationship with the board of directors. When you have so many outside investors in a hyper-growth company, everyone's expectations need to be managed.

"After I learned the Sandler sales principles, I was slow to realize that the concepts would apply to all facets of communication. For this reason, we recently made the decision to take our top-performing salespeople and start them in the Sandler leadership training. If we are to maintain this type of growth without sacrificing the culture that we worked so hard to build, we are far better off developing our management organically as opposed to bringing in outside hires. I feel good about where everything is right now."

THE EXCEPTION TO THE RULE

Mario is an amazing exception to the rule that salespeople need a fair amount of time to internalize the Sandler principles. He's living proof that some people come to these principles ready to implement them right away.

The number one question that we get from budding entrepreneurs is "When should I start hiring salespeople?" Our response is that you should not hire anyone until you can sell successfully yourself. Nothing sends a cultural message more powerfully than a leader who has walked the walk. The fact that Mario can pick up the phone at any time and make an effective sales call commands respect from his entire sales organization.

CHAPTER 5

The Fixer

CHRIS CARMOUCHE, FORMER CEO
SUNTERRA LANDSCAPE

Chris Carmouche is what you might call a "fixer." He is a super high "D" in DISC terms, meaning he tends to be quite direct and to the point. He's intense and very smart. He's the quiet guy who speaks volumes with his stare. When he took our classes, we never knew exactly how he was digesting the Sandler content until he was well into the program and started to open up a bit.

Chris purchased Sunterra Landscape with the sole intention of growing the company to sell it. This was part of a plan to invest and

> *"When all else fails, become a consultant."* —David Sandler

manage his family's money. In just nine years, with the help of our partner John Oberg, Chris and his team grew Sunterra Landscape to become one of the top 100 landscaping companies in the country and among the top 10 in Texas. In 2013, Chris sold the company, but quickly assumed the presidency of another company that he intends to grow to $100 million in five years. Judging from their most recent numbers, he is well on his way to making this happen.

WELCOME TO THE SCHOOL OF HARD KNOCKS

Chris has an interesting business background. He earned an MBA from the University of St. Thomas in Houston with a focus on technology. After graduation he took a high-tech job with a chip on his shoulder—no pun intended—and he was about to discover that he was entering the school of hard knocks. Chris was fortunate to be hired by the president of the company, a man who had an interesting training philosophy. Even though Chris had an MBA, the president treated him like he was a blank canvas. He made no assumptions about what Chris's role should be, but instead tried to give him firsthand experience about how he could best make a contribution. It's an approach that Chris has since adopted when he mentors new hires, even though he knows from direct experience that the transition can be a difficult.

Chris told us, "I showed up to my first job in a suit and tie, only to be sent home to put on jeans and a T-shirt. I was told by my boss to report to shipping and start working. Of course, this ticked me off in a major way. I did the job, but I was upset that he would start me on the ground level after all my education. Every day my manager would ask me, 'So what did you learn today?' and I would tell him everything that I saw wrong with the department. Then he told me, 'So fix the problems,' and I did. Little did I know that this was the beginning of a long journey with a common theme. I would be sent to a department, observe the operations and then fix what was wrong. This phase of my career took me to 20 cities around the world, and I learned to deal with all kinds of difficult issues. Eventually I worked my way through the entire supply chain of a multi-billion dollar company. The resentment disappeared. I felt like a hit man, and I enjoyed my job."

IN DEMAND

"After almost a decade of taking on some very challenging gigs," Chris continued, "I was being heavily recruited by major tech players. But I realized it was time for a change. I decided to purchase and run my own company. I bought Sunterra, a small landscaping firm. The move was a huge change for me. I went from managing the operations of a $26 billion high-tech company to leading a $7 million low-tech company. I wanted to buy an underperforming company in an industry that lacked sophistication. I also wanted to be in an industry where it was possible to roll competitors into my company."

We were curious about why Chris chose to work with Sandler. His response was blunt: "I knew that I needed a formalized sales process in order to grow. To be honest, I didn't care which one we installed. However, I really enjoyed my meetings with John Oberg throughout the sales process, and I wanted my people to sell like him.

"When I committed to Sandler, I made the decision to go all in. I attended all the classes for a year and studied the material. I started by sending the sales managers to both the sales and management classes. Of course, I sent the salespeople, and during the second year of the program, I decided to send most of my staff to the training. Anyone who faced a customer had to know Sandler."

At this point, we'd like to give you a little background that will illuminate how important Chris's active role in the sales training process really was. We have worked with over 200 companies, and only a select subset from within that group have overachieved. These companies were perennial INC 500 winners, were named to the *Austin Business Journal*'s "Fast 50" list, were sold for a good return on investment or met other benchmarks for high-level achievement. Perhaps you're wondering: What does this elite group of companies have in common? Their CEOs did what Chris did. They walked the talk. They personally attended the Sandler Training sessions, and they studied and used the techniques in order to lead by example. In fact, we have seen zero failures when the CEO is clearly committed.

We asked Chris, an obvious expert in process management, to explain his rollout strategy for the sales team. "I started with our funnel management," he said. "We could not budget sales, and we needed to forecast better. With a standard sales process and individual cookbooks for the sales team, we had better transparency for our sales results. Next I wanted to get the managers trained so they could hold the salespeople accountable. Then we focused on the sales team. Change is hard, so I insisted on accountability. Once I saw the changes and subsequent results, I knew that the concepts had to become even further embedded in our culture. The decision to send the rest of the company to the customer-service training was an easy one."

IN THE TRENCHES

We knew that Chris spent time in the trenches with his team on some larger opportunities. These were potential contracts with high-profile companies, deals that they ultimately won. We asked him, "Do you recall what happened in some of those deals?"

"Yes," he said, "A couple of them come to mind. The first was with a large multi-billion dollar healthcare provider. I was there with my team and was watching the meeting crash before my eyes. We were talking up a storm and had no idea what they wanted. As my guy was digging a deeper hole with all his feature-and-benefit talk, I could see that we were losing the group. I don't do this very often, but because of what was at stake I gently reached over and patted my guy's hand and interrupted him. I asked for permission to back up a bit, and I proceeded to work the conversation toward the emotionally compelling issues, or in Sandler terms, 'Pain.' Then I started to ask a lot of questions. At one point the prospect asked if we had a PowerPoint presentation. I said, 'No, we don't.' He replied quickly, 'Good, keep going!'

"As the questioning continued, we started to uncover that they wanted a much bigger solution than landscaping. They wanted more vivid colors. Why vivid color? I eventually learned that they had paid for studies that showed a positive psychological impact if the patient was surrounded by a colorful and peaceful environment. This would be hard to pull off given the location of their facilities, but fixing the colors in the patient environment was their primary pain. The color theme was to carry over into their advertising collateral in an attempt to rebrand their overall subliminal message. Had I not stopped the sales process and asked all of the questions, we never would have uncovered this information.

"The questions allowed us to co-build a solution with the customer, who became our largest client. This was a high profile, hotly contested RFP that all the major players wanted. You can't ask enough questions on a sales call. The importance of asking questions to secure this win became even more apparent to me long after we won the account. I was walking into the hospital's maternity ward with my wife, who was in labor. I paused for a moment and reflected while looking at all the flowers. They did make a positive difference, and I felt like I was part of a shared vision.

"This was a major lesson for me, as previously I had trouble asking questions and being patient enough to listen to the answers. I tended to get things done with willpower and brute force. I have been accused of leaving a high body count behind me at times. With the Sandler training and help from John, I was becoming a more balanced manager, especially with my communication.

"I have another example of a big contract win using the Sandler techniques. There is a major consumer electronics company here in Austin with a notoriously tough purchasing department. They floated an annual RFP out to numerous suppliers. In this case, we were not the incumbent supplier. Every landscape company in Texas knew that traditionally it was a million-dollar contract. That was the number that won the contract in the past: a million dollars. I was sure that the other vendors would try to sell another $1-million deal.

"Since this company was not doing well at the time, I knew that we had to do something different. Our strategy was to engineer a completely new solution. To pull this off we had to change the way the buyer was buying. We role-played as a team and spent hours planning the call. We focused especially hard on the up-front contract—the mutually agreed-upon agenda for the meeting that establishes roles and responsibilities—because if we couldn't ask a lot questions, we had no chance. When I first proposed the up-front contract, I could tell that the buyer had not heard one before. My contract probably did not come out sounding completely authentic, as I was still learning. However, to my relief, the buyer eventually opened up.

"I recall the one question that got the call moving. I asked: 'So what do you really need?' It was apparent that they needed a more basic solution than we had been envisioning. Once we changed the spec to fit their problems, we were in. In fact, the buyer did not even send our solution out for other bids. This is unheard of at this company. I'm convinced that he did not bid out the project because he sincerely trusted us. In the meantime all the other vendors provided variations of their $1-million solution. We got the deal."

A BIGGER CHALLENGE

Chris is happily married and has four great children. He has been fighting cancer, so he has a lot going on personally. We hesitated to ask him, but we wanted to know how Sandler impacted his personal life. Without hesitation, Chris said, "The techniques are permanently embedded in me. John spent a lot of extra time with me working on my emotional control while interacting with team members. As a result, I could sense my body tighten when I was getting upset, and I knew that when that happened it was time to ease up and ask more questions. Knowing this has helped me deal with the situation much more constructively. When talking to my family, I now reverse a little more—meaning I am more likely to answer a question with a question—to avoid limiting myself to a one-sided perspective. These were managerial tools when I first learned to use them, but I think that the tools are also great for my marriage and my children.

"I have a 13-year-old son, and it's pretty easy for us to butt heads. He tends to vacillate. My old strategy was to tell him, 'Get your butt moving,' in a stern tone. Now when I see that he's going to be in trouble schedule-wise due to his lack of initiative, I start to ask questions. I have found that with enough open-ended Socratic questions, he sees the light and gets moving. The beauty is that he thinks taking the initiative is all his idea!"

We asked Chris about dealing with the cancer. "I have made over 30 videos for my children. They are for the kids' weddings, my wife and their future. It's a hard thing to do. I rely on my faith and belief systems. I believe that I will live longer and this gives me the energy to run the company while remaining engaged with my family. So far I have been blessed with the good news that the cancer has stopped spreading."

CHAPTER 6

The Art of Diving In

TIM HAMILTON, CEO
PRAXENT

D avid Sandler said as much about mental toughness and growth as he did about selling tactics. He talked about having goals and building plans to reach them. He talked about having guts. He talked about failing and learning from it. He said, "Failure is universal. It's part of the human condition."

Tim Hamilton has goals and a vision. He has a plan to get there, too. As a Sandler student, he knows about failures, and

> *"Understand the process of failure and let it work." —David Sandler*

understands (to quote another David Sandler gem), "There is no growth without pain."

Tim is the 31-year-old CEO of Praxent, a multimillion-dollar web development and custom software company in Austin, Texas, with 18 employees as of this writing.

Tim started Praxent as a 16-year-old after designing a poster for a high school tennis tournament. He saw his work all over town and, from that moment forward, was hooked on graphic design. Sixteen posters later, he was asked to design a website, and he taught himself how. He had enough success that a legal association hired him to do their site. They referred him to other associations. Soon he was flying around the country managing projects while still in high school. All of a sudden, he was running a one-man business.

FRESHMAN BLUES, B-SCHOOL BREAKTHROUGH

During college, Tim kept growing his company, but had his share of failures. His dream of majoring in computer science—a key to his continued growth in web development—was shut down when he failed out of those classes in his freshman year.

Tim switched to economics and continued working on his company. He had enough success to buy a condo in his junior year and hire a full-time employee. He was rejected twice by the business school he wanted to attend, but refused to take "No" for an answer. He wrote the admissions officer a powerful letter using his business experience as a reason he should be admitted. He got in.

CODE WARS

Just as Tim fought his way into business school, he continued to build his business. He eventually landed a client who imagined a revolutionary way of organizing business in corporate America. Inspired by Wikis, the user-friendly system of web collaboration of which Wikipedia is the best-known example, this innovator approached Tim about helping him build the first iteration of tools meant to create an environment for collaboratively written documents. These tools were designed to improve workflow and increase efficiency. The system was called Open Teams. Tim labored over it for two and a half years of late nights and week-ends. At the 2007 Enterprise 2.0 Conference, his company was labeled "One of the Five Startups to Watch" as a result of this groundbreaking product. Everyone wanted to meet to discuss the product, from government agencies to Fortune 500 companies.

Despite the fact that he had written and rewritten a great piece of code, the challenge lay in getting people to buy something they liked but possibly did not fully understand. Tim and his team could not find an effective way to market it. They were competing against larger competitors and struggled with how to sell against them. He said, "We had a great piece of code and people loved the product, but we got the sales and marketing wrong. We assumed, 'If you build it they will come,' and we were wrong." He had to pay bills and employees, so he folded up Open Teams, sold it, and went after other business.

He created a new product, eCatalog, that brought transparency to the procurement process. It was adopted by the City of Houston and saved the city $20 million in its first year. Tim tried to sell it to other cities, but he lacked an effective sales process to overcome the objections of procurement officials who cared less about saving money than protecting their jobs.

Tim rebooted his company and began to grow it with a focus on websites and software. He merged with another business owner who had experience in sales, and together they grew to nine employees. After a tumultuous relationship, Tim had to sever ties as the partners had different visions of how to run the company. Tim stayed true to himself even though it meant enduring painful conflict, risking his business and losing his office, most of his employees and a lot of money. He left with two employees and started over again, working out of his condo.

CAN YOU WOW EVERY PROSPECT?

Tim tried to rebuild by working long hours, doing great work, and seeking to "wow" every prospect. He and his team prepared ad nauseam for presentations. They scrambled to make sure every detail was perfect. He was building the business, but exhausting himself and his team. He felt like he had to impress each client and offer free consulting in the selling process. That's when we met.

Hard work was only getting Tim so far. He reached out to us because he had friends who had worked with Sandler, and he heard one of our partners speak at an event. When we met, he talked about his desire to grow the business, but differently this time. He was doing OK, hovering around $1 million per year in sales, but wanted to make the sales part of the company more predictable, less painful and more efficient.

THE SANDLER DIFFERENCE

Tim began to work with Sandler Training to change the nature of his relationship with prospects.

Using Sandler principles, Tim began to take some risks and move out of his comfort zone. Rather than respond to all RFPs that came his way, he began qualifying them. Instead of doing a proposal whenever someone asked, he asked more questions to determine if the client was a fit, then he sought out agreement from prospects prior to sending over any proposal.

This is counterintuitive to most salespeople. The standard approach is to send over proposals willy-nilly without any thought to the costs involved. Working with a Sandler coach, Tim and his team took a different approach. This made working on proposals more palatable because he knew the outcome ahead of time—the prospect had already bought in and wanted to get started.

Tim also learned to push back gently and professionally when prospects or clients were in error or were trying to press for something not called for in an agreement. His business grew, but it was not without discomfort.

"It was very much a leap of faith to say some of the things that Sandler taught me," Tim recalled. "To use some of the tools that the system calls for was not easy, but I have found that there are few useful business systems out there that you can implement with complete comfort. That's not the purpose. We're not going for comfort. That's never part of the equation. I've learned that growth and comfort don't go together.

"Another profound lesson I've learned is about the nature of success. I'd thought that success would come when I had a certain amount of money. I had a fantasy that when I hit that number, I'd somehow feel secure and all my fears would go away. I imagined success would be what happened when the business crossed the million-dollar mark. That was a huge pursuit of mine; I wanted to hit a million. I didn't realize until we hit $1.5 million that the fear hadn't gone away. That's when I realized that security comes in relationships, not in money."

THE COMFORT ZONE AND THE BOTTOM LINE

We began working with Tim and his two employees in early 2010. Tim would reach out to us for help in preparing for meetings with prospects and in managing large clients. It was because of this willingness to ask for help, to try new things, and press through the discomfort that Tim and his company grew at a rapid pace. Sales have doubled twice since then.

Tim went out of his comfort zone to talk about money more with prospects. That's hard for many people, because they grow up hearing that talking about money is rude. Tim worked at having disarmingly honest conversations about money.

He also learned to set very clear customer expectations with up-front contracts about potential budget overruns, or reworks. This isn't a comfortable conversation in software, since it often happens and many sellers give up margin for fear of upsetting the client. But Tim realized he needed to address the issue up front to protect his growing company. He also needed to prevent a relationship in which clients typically asked for and received unilateral concessions. If he offered those kinds of concessions, he knew that both company morale and his bottom line would suffer greatly.

By using up-front contracts and by addressing his biggest fears (concepts he learned with Sandler), Tim built more and better relationships with clients and a workable structure for achieving shared goals.

Tim also learned when to walk away. When we met, Tim took on every scrap of business he could. Now he won't take a client who doesn't have at least a healthy five-figure budget to get started.

He's grown out of his initial office space into a much larger space and added many employees in that time. What's more, he's shifted how he thinks about the company, what roles people need to play and his own role.

WHERE, NOT HOW

Like a lot of successful entrepreneurs, Tim built and rebuilt companies multiple times and at great personal cost—financially and emotionally. One of the greatest challenges has been learning to allow others to take on some of the load of carrying the company. This is never easy for an entrepreneur, but Tim has turned the corner. He's turning over aspects of sales to other people in the company, and he's had them trained to fulfill their responsibilities. He now sees that his role isn't to do all things and be all things in this company, but to set the vision and the direction.

Tim now says his role is to answer the question, "Where?" not the question "How?" Whenever he begins to get too involved in details, his team will say, "Tim, 'where, not how.'" The exchange serves as a gentle reminder that he's there to lead, not to manage all the small details. He's hired people he trusts to do that. He holds them accountable for results, but also empowers them to get those results. That's the Sandler way.

THE VISION

Tim's strategic objective is to create a company that will be the leading provider of web cloud and mobile solutions, enhancing business performance for hundreds of clients. He plans to have 28 team members and sales of $5 million within 2 years.

When I asked Tim what drove him and what had enabled him to manage all of the setbacks he'd encountered over the years, he easily articulated the vision for his life by sharing his "non-negotiables": "My business is there to serve my life, not the other way around. My life is not there to serve my business. I need to have control of my working schedule and location. I want a collaborative environment, not a combative one. I value calm, considerate, drama-free and respectful communication in our company and with customers." This is how he's decided to operate.

Two more things: Tim has always had guts, and he's always learned from failure. Success requires both of those traits. Tim was a kid in high school when he cold called the CEO of a software development company and fought to get an unpaid internship that they didn't have. He got it. He was also in high school when he started flying around the country, doing work for legal associations. He was in college when he failed out of his chosen field, computer science. He scraped and clawed to get into a business school that had initially turned him down. He fired his first employee, saw a 2.5-year project falter for lack of experience and funds and watched his first business partnership dissolve—all before he was thirty years old. At each turn, he had the guts to persevere, learn and rebuild.

When I asked him how he managed to do so much at the age of 31, he shared a story about being a little boy scared to jump off the high dive. He'd watch all the other children jump, but when he went up there, three meters off the ground, he grew scared and climbed down, embarrassed, and sat on the edge of the pool. He got up on the board a second time and again backed down. As he watched other kids jump, he realized he could do it if he'd simply change the way he thought. Tim began re-scripting his thinking as a small boy!

He realized that he could quell the fear of jumping by not focusing on the outcome, but on the process of walking to the edge of the diving board and "taking that next step." He successfully jumped off the high dive, but he also found a way to manage fear and insecurity. To this day, when stepping into an unknown market, territory or phase of growth, he says: "Just take the next step."

CHAPTER 7

Attitude Control

COLE HARMONSON, CEO
FAR WEST CAPITAL

Cole Harmonson enjoys yoga, loves underdogs and thrives on unleashing the potential of employees, customers and entrepreneurs. He is also the CEO of Far West Capital, an asset-based lending and factoring company with 37 employees and $20 million in revenue as of this writing. Factoring, in case you're unfamiliar with the industry, is the practice of a company selling its outstanding invoices, at a discount, to a third party (the factor) who then has the right to collect the amount owed.

> *"You can't accomplish anything great by playing it safe."* —David Sandler

Cole grew up in Lubbock, Texas, where entrepreneurship and sales became part of his DNA at an early age. His father was the number one salesperson for Xerox one year, then left to start a business of his own and went on to start several more. Cole worked in a few of those businesses and learned about selling and running a company firsthand.

"YOU CAN'T DO THAT"

After graduating from Texas Tech with a degree in finance, Cole took an entry-level job with a local bank. He was drawn immediately to the factoring group, because he wanted to put together and sell deals—something not everyone at the bank wanted to do. What's more, with a wife and two small children to support, he was motivated by the income opportunity that selling offered.

But there was a problem. Cole's supervisors told him he couldn't work in factoring for at least three years. He labored in the credit department for almost 18 months, until he found a better opportunity. He was asked to move to Ft. Worth to run marketing for a bank. He said, "Yes"—and became a VP of Marketing at the age of 24. He still wanted to work in factoring, so he started a factoring product for the bank and then closed a few deals.

The bank's leadership didn't truly understand the factoring

business, but Cole did, and the die was cast. Cole understood the difference between traditional banking and factoring, and he wanted to factor. After seven months at the bank, frustrated by the lack of desire to grow the factoring business he encountered from the bank's leadership, he left.

He joined Don Stricklin, the 36-year-old CEO of State Bank in a small town one hour east of Austin. Cole was straightforward about his professional objectives. He wanted to factor. Don told him, "You have two rules: Make money and don't lose money. If you follow those, we'll get along just fine."

HIGHS AND LOWS

Over the next 11 years, Cole followed both rules. He grew the factoring and asset-based lending (ABL) department from zero to $50 million and expanded the staff from only himself to 22 employees. He sold deals, took care of customers and built his team. When he joined the bank in 1996, it had $73 million in assets and one location. When the bank was sold in 2007, it boasted $2 billion and 41 locations.

When the company was sold, Cole wanted to buy the factoring and asset-based lending portfolio. His plan was to open the doors on day one with $50 million in the portfolio. His first choice for a partner, Don, couldn't partner with him since he sat on the board of the now-public State Bank. Cole found another partner to go in with him to acquire the portfolio, which he regarded as his business and looked forward to continuing to manage.

A few days before the deal was to close, he learned that his new partner intended to sell the portfolio as soon as they acquired it. Cole refused to sell. The partner sued and Cole reluctantly sold the portfolio he had worked so hard to build to a different bank—then went to work for the acquiring bank.

CULTURE CLASH—AND THE BIRTH OF A NEW COMPANY

The solution to the partnership crisis brought along its own problems. Within just two months Cole saw that the values he held dear—honoring your word, serving customers, working with integrity—conflicted with the priorities of the new bank's leadership. He had said he could keep customers 50% longer and charge 25% more than the competition. He'd been doing it for 11 years and had built the portfolio that way. Management didn't believe him. After two months on the job, Cole took two weeks off to reflect on what he wanted and where he was headed.

At the end of that two weeks, he decided that his values were incompatible with theirs, and that he could not live his values in that environment. Thirty days after joining the bank, Cole chose to quit and strike out on his own.

In late 2007, Cole wrote a check to start Far West Capital. Even before the paperwork was done, he had customers waiting for him. Don, his boss at State Bank, resigned from the board of the bank and joined him as a partner. Former employees left what they were doing to work with him again. His company was growing well in late 2009 when we connected. (That was sixteen months after our first cold call to Cole!)

HOW DO YOU SCALE RELATIONSHIP BUILDING?

Cole had come to a place in his business where he knew he wanted to keep growing, but realized the growth would take him beyond what he could do alone. He could sell and provide great service—offering a trusted-advisor type of relationship—but he could only sell and service so many accounts. To grow the company as he had built it, he had to find a system to replicate his own innate abilities across the company.

We began working together because Cole wanted to "scale relationship building." Where he was strong—selling and taking care of customers—he needed everyone else to be great, as well. He didn't have a means of imparting his own skills to his team. Like many entrepreneurs/leaders, he was unconsciously competent, but couldn't explain what he was doing or why it worked so well. It was just what he did.

First and foremost, Cole took the Sandler training himself. He discovered that a lot of what he'd been doing for years matched well with Sandler philosophically. The training simply gave him language for what already worked for him, as well as a process for managing client and prospect interactions.

Next, he began to train his management and sales teams in the Sandler Selling System. He did this because he wanted them using the same processes and methodology he'd been learning.

Finally, the company began training all operations team members. Why? Cole wanted the communication that the sales and management team used with clients to be consistent throughout the company. One of Far West Capital's goals is 100% happy clients. Much of that happiness depended on staff understanding clients better, hearing them out and communicating more effectively.

CULTURALLY EMBEDDED

Sandler became culturally embedded at Far West Capital and is the central component of the company's work culture today. The Far West Capital sales team uses up-front contracts at every meeting. Sales and operations people are always asking prospects and clients, "What is the real issue? What is the pain we can help you address?" Because Far West Capital team members follow a process, they know why they lose deals when it happens.

When we asked Cole about his approach to development, he said, "I see this like karate or yoga—you don't graduate. You'd never stop marketing, so why stop training? There's always more to learn."

The Far West Capital team applies the Sandler concept of the "cookbook" (a preplanned list of prospecting behaviors that one must do in order to be successful) to every aspect of revenue: marketing, sales and account management. They stay focused and disciplined on their key activities while taking great care of clients.

WHAT'S THE SECRET?

Currently, Far West Capital is rapidly outpacing more established factoring companies. Banks often ask, "Why are you growing so much faster than your competition?" Cole attributes it to their culture and the way they take care of clients. Turnover is extremely low, and recently the company was voted one of the best places to work in Texas.

What's more, that culture has attracted top talent. Recently, a salesperson joined the team after having interviewed with someone from operations. The new salesperson felt certain he could count on outstanding service to back up what he sold because his interviewer, who wasn't even a salesperson, knew more about clients and their motivations than salespeople would at competing companies.

As a result of Sandler Training, Cole has seen clients open up more as the whole team focuses on listening more intently, asking better questions and being more proactive in all facets of the relationship.

GROWTH ISSUES

As Far West Capital grew, its sales became more than Cole could oversee personally. What had been Cole and 7 clients had grown to 37 employees and 253 clients. Somewhere well before 253 clients, Cole realized he couldn't sell, be CEO and also manage the sales team. First he let go of selling, prospecting and relationship building—others would have to do that. It was uncomfortable, but he chose to have faith in the processes he'd built, the people they'd hired and the product they offered their clients. The sales team thrived.

His next major growth milestone was letting go of sales management. He promoted a very capable team member to EVP to run sales and marketing. While Cole is strong in both those areas, he knew that the growth of the company demanded that he focus on the vision, mission and culture and let other people—maybe even people more capable than himself in certain areas—run key parts of the company.

CHANGE IS GOOD, GROWTH IS GOOD

We asked him, "Why, when you were doing so well, did you begin to make changes?"

He replied, "Just because something works doesn't mean there's not a better way. I knew what I was doing myself couldn't get me where we could go. So I sought out Sandler. I've always believed in breaking it before it needs to be broken. It will break—but will it be on purpose or because we weren't able to handle what the business demanded?" He realized that he had to give up something—in this case, some measure of control—to gain something greater: a bigger, stronger, healthier company.

When we asked what Cole had to do to grow himself and the company, he said, "I had to put my ego aside and not make it about me." He focuses a great deal on personal growth and, as a result, the company grows as people follow his lead. Cole believes, "If I'm not stretching myself and growing, how can I lead others?" When we asked him how he grew on a personal level, he said, "I have to keep pushing my comfort zone. That's where the growth is."

The key to his growth has been the attitudes he's maintained throughout the years, despite the setbacks he's endured: not being able to buy the factoring division; getting sued; and working with a bad company. He doesn't dwell on the negative, but sees opportunity everywhere. The same mindset that allows him to charge more and keep customers longer also enables him to see adversity as a good thing and not give in to fear. He's a model of what David Sandler taught in many ways:

- He has goals that he writes down every day—daily, short-term and long-term.
- He meets with others who can support him in pursuit of his goals.
- He expects good things to happen and is a mental winner.
- He keeps a journal and writes in it daily, starting with a gratitude list.
- He has the guts to face adversity.
- He makes business interactions about others as opposed to himself. His mentality is that if you fill the other guy's basket to the brim because it's the right thing to do, you attract good people, good customers and better results.
- He identifies what is out of his control and doesn't worry

about those things. Instead, he focuses on what he can control.

- He does the things he's uncomfortable doing, and they have become assets for him.

Cole believes, "Change happens incrementally and slowly, over time, with persistence and intent. There have been many situations for me—like getting sued—that I thought were bad that were actually good in the end. So I've always had a perspective that if it's happening, it must be for my good. That's been the key."

CHAPTER 8

*Freedom, Stability
and Equal Partners*

LEIGHTON HENDRICK
INDEPENDENT MARKETING CONSULTANT

W hile thinking of who to interview for this book, we decided that it would be interesting to reconnect with some people we trained more than five years ago. One former client, Blue Fish Development Group, immediately came to mind. Blue Fish is an innovative and creative company with one of the best corporate cultures we've ever seen. Unfortunately, they were in a tough situation at the time their management reached out to us.

> *"You never have to like prospecting; you just have to do it."* —David Sandler

The platform for which the team was developing software became outdated almost overnight. As a result, sales were crashing. It was as if Blue Fish had been a developer for Apple and overnight Apple had vanished. It was a dark period in the company's history.

The CEO, Michael Trafton, asked everyone to help with sales. In an effort to save the company, his plan was to initiate an all-out assault on sales, starting with an aggressive prospecting plan. Every employee, no matter the job title, was asked to help find any remaining holdout companies that were still using the old platform. To complicate matters, the economy had just begun to descend into the Great Recession. Budgets were being slashed.

This brings us to Leighton Hendrick. She worked in marketing for Blue Fish Development Group and had never sold before, but she stepped forward and volunteered to make prospecting calls. When we assessed her, all the indications were that cold calling would cause her a heavy dose of emotional anguish. In spite of our recommendation to pass on the assignment, Leighton stood firm. She wanted to hit the phones. We remember being amazed that she was willing to start the training. We were even more amazed that she was soon making at least 50 cold calls a day.

AN EARLY START

Leighton is a native Texan who grew up in a small Texas town. She is outgoing, gregarious and, surprisingly for a Texan, a dedicated surfer. Leighton frequently travels for surfing, in search, she told us, of "the perfect wave," but she does not embody that laid-back spirit in her professional life. She's all business, having graduated from the University of Texas with a degree in communications and started her career quite early, at the height of the dot-com boom. The business environment was growing so rapidly back then that some students were being recruited as early as their sophomore year. Leighton was one of them.

After graduation, Leighton had numerous job offers that would have taken her outside of Texas, but in the end she decided to stay closer to home by taking a job with Trilogy, a legendary Austin startup. Her job eventually migrated to a recruiting position on college campuses hiring students for development and consulting roles. The recruiting results of the department were so good that Trilogy spun off this division in order to sell recruiting services to other companies.

This new environment was not ideal for Leighton. The increased focus on sales made her feel uncomfortable. She decided to move to another startup and took a job in marketing—just in time for the dot-com crash.

COLD CALLS?

Like a great surfer, Leighton rode that wave as long as possible, getting laid off at least five times as the high-tech companies she joined quickly closed. Leighton was addicted to the risk and the raw energy of startups. When there were no more attractive start-ups for which to apply, she landed at Blue Fish in the marketing department. That takes us back to the cold-call mission.

The first question we asked Leighton was how she felt after volunteering to make calls only to learn afterward that she did not assess well for sales, but found herself in our class anyway. She admitted, "I was terrified to say the least. I literally felt sick to my stomach. The only reason that I kept my commitment was because I wanted to help my fellow teammates at Blue Fish. I felt completely intimidated and agreed with the assessment that I had a massive need for approval and a problem talking about money. My major issue was that I wanted to be liked by every-body. Rejection wipes me out.

"Intellectually, I understood the Sandler cold-call process, but emotionally I was struggling with it. I remember being so con-flicted. I'm a friendly person and like to talk most of the time. My belief was that the more I talked, the greater the odds I would be liked; if I was liked, I would get the sale. If I was liked, people wouldn't yell at me. That's what I believed. The fact is that in the hundreds of calls I made, I only got yelled at once. On the other hand, I was not getting results.

"Eventually I started to use the Sandler prospecting process, as opposed to just understanding it. The first time that it worked I started to buy in and feel more comfortable."

GATEKEEPER BLUES

"Even though I was using the system," Leighton recalls, "I still struggled with gatekeepers and the ensuing wrestling match as I tried to get through to the decision maker. As luck would have it, my mom was an executive assistant. I asked her about salespeople who called and how she handled them. She said that she hated the representatives who pretended to be her friends by using fake sincerity in hopes of getting sent through. She ditched those people. She preferred sales professionals who were honest and straightforward with her. I could see how what she was telling me tied into Sandler's concept of the up-front contract."

Leighton was a fixture at our prospecting labs—optional sessions at our training center where students can make cold calls under the coaching eyes of our trainers. She was not having much luck setting meetings, but she was performing more than her fair share of the Sandler behaviors. In other words, she was making more calls than she was being asked to do, in spite of all the discomfort.

We asked Leighton when she started to gain traction. She said, "I recall one of the first times that I was passed through to the executive by the gatekeeper. I was so excited at first, but then started to panic because I had no idea of what to say when I got through! This was a complex technical sale and there was no way that I could carry on a technical conversation with a prospect. Of course I stumbled through my up-front contract. I was so bad that he said, 'Let me help you.'

"I had to fight the urge to share lots of product knowledge

when he asked me questions. In spite of my naiveté and nervousness, the prospect was more than willing to help me through the call. He rescued me. Looking back, he probably sensed how 'not-OK' I was feeling. I remembered the principles I had been taught in class and the internal conflict I had with the idea of acting like I didn't know the answer. It seemed to me that I was being dishonest by pretending not to know something. Intellectually, I felt that it was insincere. However, when I was in the situation with the executive, I was naturally sincere and it worked. In hindsight, that was another example of my high need for approval. I felt that he would like me more if I knew all the answers to his questions."

MOVING BEYOND A NEED FOR APPROVAL

We pressed Leighton about the genesis of her need for approval. She got quiet and then shared that the combination of her upbringing and her own observations of the community where she was raised indicated a predictable sequence of expected life events for her gender: Be a good little girl. Get good grades. Get married. Be a good mother.

To complicate matters, Leighton's parents divorced when Leighton was in fifth grade. She found herself separated from her brother and father. She said, "All these factors shaped me as a person who wanted to please people and be liked. At the same time, deep down, I wanted to live my own life—and that did not fit the mold in which I was raised.

"All of these feelings came to the forefront as I began to journal.

I was hurting from all the rejection of the sales calls. One of the biggest issues that I had to overcome was bailing whenever the conversations about the prospect's issues became too serious. My logic was that people should know how they felt about an issue and that it was not my job to uncover those details. In other words, I did not want the conversation to get into personal pain. Obviously, this was a roadblock. I was deep in my journal every day, dealing with all the issues that were giving me all these problems."

MONEY TALK

"In my journaling," Leighton continued, "it also became clear that I hated to talk about money. I grew up in a family that had plenty of money until my parents' divorce. Then Mom and I struggled. Money became a taboo topic, and I did everything that I could to avoid the subject."

Leighton left the Blue Fish Development Group to start her own marketing firm, a job that would require her to sell and discuss money. We asked, "So how do you handle the budget conversation now?"

"I would panic when they asked my rate and hated to answer that question," she answered. "I would choke out '$75/hour,' though I'm sure my body language and flushed complexion gave away my discomfort. Finally, out of frustration, I figured that I would reverse the question. When one president asked me, 'So what's your rate?' I replied, 'That's a good question. What are you accustomed to paying?' He told me the he paid between $100 and

$125 per hour. I simply said that was in line with my range. That one simple question gave me a raise and relieved all of my stress!

"There were situations where the rate would come up and the prospect would gawk at the number. One time, out of frustration, I went more negative than he did by saying, 'If you are uncomfortable with the rate, would it make sense to end the meeting early?' He replied 'Yes.' I remember how psyched I was! I got out of the meeting early so I could take on other tasks. As a bonus, I didn't have to argue about the rate. I can't explain how good I felt after that moment.

"I wish I had tried that earlier. I still have money issues, but between the journaling and the Sandler tools, I can now relax a little more on my sales calls. Most importantly, I started to look at the selling process as an activity that is not about me. In fact, I am the least important person on the sales call!"

PAYING IT FORWARD

Leighton recalled how she referenced Sandler when volunteering to do some fundraising work. "Of all people, I was the one who found myself coaching others on how to ask for money for a charity I support. Who likes asking for money? To help everyone relax, I trained them to go for the *no*. I made it a game. I offered a free dinner to anyone who was told, 'No.' I had one rule—they had to ask for the money. I did not have to give out a single free dinner."

Leighton chose to bring up her personal life and some of the changes she consciously made as a result of the Sandler training.

Reflecting back on her early life, she remembered how she had been expected to live according to a "template" that was largely defined by her mother. Gradually, as her need for approval waned, she started to be more assertive about living her life with a "new template." Her need for approval was telling her to comply with the old messages from her childhood, but she was not obeying them. We could see a new freedom shining in Leighton's eyes.

As our interview drew to a close, we asked if Leighton could share any lessons that would be important to aspiring Sandler students. She thought for a moment, then recalled, "I once had a demanding and unreasonable client. He broke every up-front contract with me. He was rude and a real pain. One day I built up the guts to tell him, 'Look, I have presented my deliverables. I get the feeling that even if I accomplish all of them, you still won't be happy with my work.' Do you know what he said? 'Yes, you're right.'

"I told him calmly, 'This is not a fit,' and ended the relationship. There is no way that my former need for approval would have allowed me to say those words."

Leighton's is not the unreachable fantasy story of the salesperson who made a zillion dollars, although she certainly is successful. She is a unique person who has been able to refine her life and create a balanced environment where there is less stress and self-doubt. Those changes are priceless.

CHAPTER 9

Starting Small, Thinking Big

RYAN JASKIEWICZ, CEO
12FIVE CAPITAL

R yan Jaskiewicz is the CEO of 12five Capital, a commercial finance company based in Chicago, Illinois. He grew up around financing, watching his father work and hearing about how deals were put together. He found the world of business fascinating from a young age and would go into the office with his dad on Saturdays and during the summers.

After putting himself through college with a boat-detailing business, Ryan worked as a bartender for a while and pondered his

> *"Decide what you want, build a plan, and you can bet on the outcome."* —David Sandler

next move. His father told him how exciting the finance industry was at the time. (This was before the Great Recession.) Business was so hot that his dad's company was able to turn down deals if they weren't big enough. Anything less than $50,000 a month got tossed. Ryan, however, saw an opportunity in those smaller deals.

He knew he didn't have to make a lot of money, as he was young and single. He also realized he might be able to charge customers a small premium because larger companies didn't want their deals. He wrote a business plan and showed it to his father, who thought it was a good idea. That's all he needed to hear.

THINK SMALL

Ryan financed the business by seeking out wealthy investors to capitalize his small operation. After eight in a row had turned him down, he found one person willing to lend him $100,000. He used that capital to finance four $25,000 deals. Shortly thereafter he began paying his investor interest and word got around. Soon other investors lined up to lend him money. Then his father's firm started throwing all the small deals it received to Ryan's company. He was on his way.

For three years, like so many entrepreneurs, Ryan did everything himself. He sold, marketed and managed the transactions, operations and all aspects of customer service. In the early days, he kept his day job bartending until a steady stream of revenue was coming in. Some nights, he would bartend until 3:00 a.m., wake up early, put on his suit and meet with bankers or investors at 8:00 a.m. He worked long days, 10 to 12 hours, sometimes 16.

By his third year in business, the economy had tanked and there wasn't a lot of money to do deals. Sometimes he'd spend the entire day looking for investors. Despite the downturn, by 2010, he had grown his portfolio to $500,000. Like many business owners we work with, he knew that if he wanted to make some real money, he'd have to scale up. So he took a risk and asked his father to come work for him and help sell. After two weeks of thinking about it, his father agreed. Soon his father began making more than Ryan paid himself, but less than he had earned at his prior employer.

THE MILLION-DOLLAR BREAKTHROUGH

While hiring his dad helped grow the company, it didn't provide as much growth as Ryan had hoped. He and his father had their share of problems, especially when one person wanted to finance a deal and the other didn't, and there was commission on the line. However, they worked through it by clarifying roles, setting boundaries and adjusting compensation to align with everyone's best interests.

Ryan was eager to grow the business when we met in 2012. He had made the tough choice to hire more people and work to bring in new business, rather than wait for the money to come in before staffing up. He knew that to grow he needed sales training, and, on the recommendation of a mentor, he chose to work with us.

Ryan told us, "I had never taken a sales training course, and that made it nerve-wracking. The training was a lot of money at the time, but we took the plunge and I went full force into Sandler. When I decide to do something, I go in 100%. I listened to the MP3s all day. I went to all of my training classes, rarely missed participating and practiced a lot. Just by doing that, we added a million dollars in business in the next year. We put out a million dollars more in deals—about $300,000 over the year in additional revenue, which was great! Sandler gave me a mindset that I could buy into fully. The concepts spoke to me because the sales processes are based on how people tick."

CHANGING THE INTERNAL CONVERSATION

Ryan not only learned how to sell more effectively, but also how to build, implement and adjust a plan for growth. His thinking shifted from, "I need to do these deals or I won't make money," to "All I can control is my own activity." The change took time, but he'd build his cookbook, work it for thirty days and track its effectiveness. If it worked, he stuck with it. If it didn't, he adjusted it.

Ryan's perspective and attitudes changed over his first year working with Sandler. He told us, "I began to change my internal conversations and tell myself that I was financially independent. I convinced myself that I didn't need certain deals and would not beg for them. Instead I went into meetings saying, 'If I can help you, I will. If I can't, that's no big deal.'

"That attitude transitioned into my daily life as well. I have always been big on both physical and mental health, and I realized that I needed to delegate some duties. When we started making money and had a lot more work to do, I hired another person. Now we had someone to manage our pipeline.

"As deals came in, she was working them, while we were focused not only on current deals, but getting new deals in the pipeline instead of having to scramble for them. Growth was exciting, but it put a lot on my plate and I had to focus mentally. I started spending time with myself every morning. I did a minimum of 20 minutes of meditation, as well as journaling and doing affirmations.

"I always had goals and knew them well, but writing them down made a big difference. When I started writing mine, it was like magic. That one activity was a huge influence on my life and career."

Ryan's company, when we interviewed him, had five employees including him. He's aiming for nine by the end of 2016, with a net funds employed goal of $10 million. That's doubling the previous year. It sounds like a big number, but it's actually doing what they've been doing and focusing on not losing existing clients. Ryan believes it can be done without sacrificing everything else that's important to him. Now he has the tools and systems to help him get there in a healthy, balanced way. But it wasn't always so.

BURNING THE CANDLE AT BOTH ENDS

Ryan told us, "You have to take care of your mind, body and spirit, but in business too often we don't address that. Most entrepreneurs—and those who work for them—feel that they must work relentless hours. They don't think about what they are doing to their bodies until they are exhausted, burnt out or can afford to hire an expensive coach to tell them what their mothers said when they were kids: 'Get a full night's sleep!' Instead too many people grind out 16-hour days, week after week. That is not sustainable or productive. For me, simple physical things like running every day and eating healthy always came easy. Then I got busy building a business and let sleep lose its priority."

Ryan began working more and putting in longer hours. He wanted to deliver on exceptional customer service, and he wanted to win business. This came at a price, especially as the company grew in headcount and revenue. He'd work till six or seven at night, and then bring his laptop home to work even more.

More and more, he saw that he was present at home physically, but not in other ways. By now, Ryan had a wife and young daughter. He was stealing time from those he loved most, and he didn't want to damage those relationships. Eventually, he chose to do things differently.

AIMING HIGH, MAINTAINING BALANCE

"When we had our daughter," Ryan told us, "my wife and I put barriers in place to shield our family time from business demands.

We decided that family and parenting issues came first and drew a clear line between work and family. If someone tries to pressure us to cross that line, we don't react. We just pull back. We make sure that our personal time is number one because if the family doesn't work, nothing works.

"To spend time with my family and grow my business in a healthy way, I had to learn to work smarter and not waste time. I block my time carefully and follow a task list every day. I manage what I can manage and, if I can't manage it, I hire somebody to do some of my work. It's worth paying an extra fifty grand so I can get home at 5:00 or 5:30 and play with my kid, be there for bath time and not miss dinner ever. I think that having quality personal time is a Generation Y value, and it's a good one.

"I want to enjoy my family and make money. I think there is a way to do both without having to work fifteen hours a day. I think I can make a million dollars a year working eight hours a day. I believe that is possible if you have the right mindset and stick to it."

Ryan learned to build this attitude into how he managed clients and their needs: "I must manage my clients' expectations. They understand that they are not going to get ahold of me after 6:00 p.m. They might as well leave a message. No one is going to die if I don't call back until the morning. If that means I lose out on a deal, I lose one. There will be another deal that works within the framework I have set."

THE RETENTION CHALLENGE

"Another key piece of growth," Ryan notes, "is keeping customers longer. When I started with Sandler, I believed that clients were going to stay for about 12 months. In our industry, companies tend to lose most clients in about a year, but that is often a self-fulfilling prophecy. And I hate doing more sales than I have to! If I can keep clients happy and have them on board for another year, that means I'm doubling my sales.

"Over the last year, I've seen a major change. Clients are staying for at least 24 months, and we're not doing anything differently in terms of the service we provide. We always treated our clients very well. Now we have changed our expectation of how long they will stay with us. We treat them like nobody else is treating their clients and try to keep them for 18 months or 24 months and get them to renew with us for at least one year. We've got clients who have renewed with us for four or five years."

IDENTITY AND ROLE

One reason for his success is that Ryan has grown in terms of separating his identity from his role. It's easy for business owners and executives to equate business success and failure with their personal value. By understanding Sandler's I/R theory, which distinguishes between the role we play at any given moment and our identity as a human being, Ryan began to realize that losing deals wasn't the end of the world. He also concluded that if other people tried unethical practices, it wasn't a personal attack on him. These internal breakthroughs led to fewer stressful nights at home and a greater enjoyment of the business.

In short, Ryan has been a model Sandler student. He has applied the principles across all areas of his life, working on his behaviors as a seller and manager, refining his techniques in selling and remaining constantly aware of his attitudes toward his customers, employees and himself. At the same time, he has built a strong, growing business with an ambitious plan of expansion, while being fully committed to a family life that gives him joy and balance.

·

CHAPTER 10

Why Be Desperate for a Bad Deal?

BURKE KENNEDY, PRINCIPAL
AVISON YOUNG

urke Kennedy is a commercial real estate broker, with a concentration on office tenant representation. He does well at it. He's affable, warm and well-versed in a number of topics, ranging from sports to history to business. He carved out a name for himself in Austin's highly competitive real estate market before the age of 35.

When he was growing up, everyone told Burke he should sell for a living. He didn't see that career in himself, but decided to give

"There is no growth without pain." —*David Sandler*

it a shot anyway. His father sold and did so successfully, so Burke thought maybe it was genetic. Maybe he could produce success solely by virtue of his DNA. It turned out that a gift for selling is not inherited. Burke hated the job. Most of all, he hated the crass attitude he felt he was expected to adopt—overcome every objection, push, close hard, take what you want and focus on the sale, not the client. Everything about that kind of selling turned him off.

Burke said, "I was taught to sell the old-fashioned way: Get the business no matter what. I just couldn't do it that way. It's not who I am or who I want to be. I couldn't get over the mental hump that demanded constant perfection. It was an all-or-nothing attitude. You are either 100% or you're 0%. At some level, I knew that didn't make sense, but it was the prevailing culture at my firm.

"The more experienced brokers had a large client base and were not selling in the real sense of the word, but new brokers were forced to go out and sell with no mentoring. If I could have observed veteran brokers selling, I might have felt differently. Instead I came back day after day feeling that I had failed. I failed. I failed. I failed. That negativity completely ripped away any confidence I had in selling."

DISSATISFACTION—AND A CHANGE IN COURSE

As a junior associate, Burke didn't control his relationship with clients. He was 100% dependent upon senior brokers for new business. The clients they gave him determined the size of his commission. While he disliked feeling dependent on others, he didn't have the skills and confidence to win his own clients. He didn't want to cold call because if he had no success, he knew he would hear about his failure back at the office.

Burke still has strong feelings about those days. He told us, "Criticism is useless unless it gives you practical ideas on how to get better. Non-stop negative feedback doesn't make you want to go out and do it again. Not only are you getting kicked in the head by secretaries, office administrators and the occasional prospect, but you are coming back with bad news and getting kicked in the head again by people on your team. The sales world didn't agree with me. I was not doing well, so I felt that I must be in the wrong field. I didn't see that I brought value to the company, even though, deep down, I knew I did a great job for my clients because of the service I was providing. I knew that in my heart of hearts. It just wasn't netting any kudos in the office or any major commissions.

"I was in bad shape. Others told me I wasn't succeeding, but no external criticism could match the critic in my head. My self-esteem was at rock bottom, and I felt like a failure. I'd been dating the woman I loved for six years, but didn't feel I could marry her because my career was still up in the air. I was afraid to move ahead with my life.

"I realized that I had no control over my own destiny. I was merely a glorified administrative assistant getting dragged around by senior brokers. I didn't know how to sell, I got punished for not knowing how to sell, and yet no one would teach me how to get better. Selling was a negative experience even though I was making decent money for someone a few years out of college. One day, I just couldn't take it anymore. Despite being on track for my first six-figure-income year, I made a decision to take control of my life. After three years as a broker, I applied to law school.

"I had a positive feeling about the law as I had grown up around a lot of lawyers. My dad is an attorney who ended up going into commercial real estate. I looked at the attorneys I grew up around and realized that all of them knew how to speak well. These lawyers were not only articulate, but also smart and curious—all the attributes I wanted. And they were confident. I asked myself, 'How can I get what they've got?' I figured it had to be law school.

"Once I was accepted, I told myself, *This is what I'm doing. I'm going to plant the flag and go forward.* I started out doing very well in school and was in the top 5% my first year. I could gradually taper off studying and have some fun in law school as opposed to the drudgery I'd felt in sales."

Burke finally married his college sweetheart between his second and third years of law school. He had lost his fear of speaking in public, and no longer felt others were judging him. His skin thickened, and his confidence grew. As a result, he did well in his studies and had great success in moot court, so much so that people told him he should become a trial attorney. When he asked his colleagues why they thought he was so good in court, they said, "Because you're so great at selling!" He started to believe he could sell—while in law school.

A SETBACK

Burke said, "I knew I had the background to be a good salesperson, and I didn't want to sit in a law office all day. I wanted to be out meeting people. Somehow I started to believe I might be able to sell after all, so I returned to the commercial real estate firm I'd left three years earlier with a new positive attitude and more skills. This time I was sure that things would be different. They weren't. Soon I started to feel my newfound confidence slip away. Once again, I felt I had to be perfect and do things like the other brokers. I saw my hard-won sense of control start to disappear.

"Even though I was working under a different broker, I was dealing with the same old attitude: 'You are always at my beck and call. I'm giving you so many projects that you don't have time to go out and sell on your own; at the same time, I expect you to go out and sell on your own. One more thing: I'm not going to teach you how to go out and sell on your own.'

"I talked to my brother and told him that maybe I should quit and become a lawyer after all. I knew what a bad selling experience did to me the first time around, and I didn't want to go through that again. Even my wife said, 'Maybe this isn't the best idea.' Thank goodness, that's when I ran into Sandler."

THE TURNING POINT

The CEO of Burke's company came to an event we held and decided to engage Market Sense, Inc., the local Sandler Training center, to work with his team. Burke was skeptical.

"I thought it was going to be the same old two-day sales training where they asked ridiculous questions like, 'When you meet with a prospect, which direction are your feet pointing under the table? If they point out, then you're a good salesperson, but if they point in, you don't have confidence.' I was afraid Sandler was going to tell me, 'This is how you sell. Why aren't you doing it this way? Stand up. Now sell me.' I didn't want to go in and hard sell anybody. Fortunately I'd come to the right place."

Burke began to train with Sandler. When we asked him why he stayed with us, he said, "I knew I could succeed in commercial real estate, and Sandler seemed to have a different way of selling that agreed with my own style. I could see that I had been using Sandler's methods when I was selling at my best. I just didn't realize I could use those principles all the time. When I came back, the first two deals I got at Commercial Texas resulted from calling old clients, renewing old relationships and saying, 'I don't know if you're ready to go through this process yet, but I'm happy to help you when you are. Please reach out to me when you're comfortable.' They surprised me by saying, 'I want to sign up with you.' I said to myself, *You mean, I don't need to put my pen on the letter of authorization and slide it over the desk?*"

In the Sandler Selling System, Burke found a way of selling that made sense to him. He recalls, "The class on pain was the first one I attended. I thought it was amazing. I didn't have to do a song and dance for an hour while the client glazed over as I went through a hundred things we could do for them that had nothing to do with their needs. Sandler told me that when I'm selling and clients say 'no,' it's because they don't need my services instead of my having done something wrong. That was a new concept. Suddenly I began to understand that selling is about clients and their needs. It's not about me. Why didn't I see that before? It was so different than what I'd been doing. I didn't want to do it the old way anymore. The Sandler way took less of my time, it took less of the client's time and it got to a decision point in no time. It was all about decision points.

"I thought Sandler was great. It just clicked for me. I saw that my desire had been so low because of how awful the old win-or-lose style of selling had been for me. The Sandler folks made it simpler and more honest. Just do what you do, and here are some techniques to help you succeed. This was wonderful."

TAKING A STAND

Burke also became more confident in standing up to prospects. He recalled, "I was asking a prospect for a letter of authorization. We don't work without a letter of authorization, even though the paper is about as legally binding as signing a napkin. They can rip it up at any time and we're not coming after them. But it gives us something of a commitment that almost all companies honor and some measure of security that they're not working with someone else.

"My prospect sent me an email that said, 'Our company policy is not to sign binding contracts, but please put together a list of properties, tour us through them and negotiate our lease. Trust us.' I couldn't believe he felt he could treat us like that, but maybe some desperate salesperson had trained him how to treat us. I wasn't buying it. I responded in my email, 'No, we won't do it.' In the last line, I wrote, 'We want to work with you, but we understand if your company policy prevents it. Please let us know if you have any questions.' I was no longer desperate for a bad deal! I loved feeling that I had equal business stature with my prospects and that my company and I had rights."

As a result of feeling more comfortable, Burke's attitude changed and he was more willing to prospect. In fact, he became a prospecting animal, meeting with people all the time. He realized that any one person could lead him to the next big deal. He just had to keep meeting lots of people. While his initial method of prospecting was a shotgun approach, it worked. It gave him momentum. To his surprise, he started having a lot of fun.

Now Burke says, "My confidence became sky high. I could go into any meeting and didn't push back or go into the old hard sell. With a new attitude and better selling techniques, along with making more and more sales calls, I had more confidence. The more confident I became the better I was at selling. I also discovered that I would rather sell in person than any other way. I learned that's where I'm most effective."

MANAGEMENT BUYS IN

Burke's sales manager bought into Sandler's approach as well and wanted to incentivize the behaviors he'd learned. He created a prospecting contest and allowed the participants to pick the awards. Since the sales cycle can be so long in commercial real estate, he wanted to keep them motivated and didn't blink when they chose a trip to Europe as first prize. Burke won the contest easily. Not only did he win the trip, he began to see commissions roll in. Just 12 months after working with Sandler, Burke's production was up 75% over his best year. This year, Burke is on pace to double that number.

PROSPECTING DAY BY DAY

He continues to practice the concepts Sandler taught him. He looks for people he can talk to wherever he may be. He chose not to take a parking spot in the company garage so he can park a block or two from the office and meet people along the way. He spends a lot of time in the morning at coffee shops because he can meet people there, too. He reasons, "No one walks into my office asking for help with commercial real estate. I need to go find them."

Burke works hard at being consistent, and he knows that's where it's easiest to get discouraged. Even though he's had some success, he says, "The hardest thing for me is to keep going when I'm not seeing immediate results. My sales manager has been good at telling me, 'Here's your suspect list. You just have to talk to 12 people a week.' I think that sounds doable." Burke would try to schedule 12 lunches, coffees or breakfasts each week. He'd reach out to his contacts, call on people and leverage his business networks to get 12 new meetings.

Burke said, "So I make 12 calls and none of them calls me back. I make 12 more calls and none of them responds, either. Instead of going into that old negative self-talk, I try to stay focused on talking to more people. That keeps me looking for that one who will want my help.

"Even with the best training, sales is hard; it ebbs and flows. But now I'm no longer at the mercy of someone else to hand me a deal. I'm not selling like a person I wouldn't buy from. I'm back in control of my life, as well as my deals, and I feel good about that."

CHAPTER 11

Not Playing the Child Anymore

JEFF MARROW, PRESIDENT
PERCOLATOR LETTERPRESS COMPANY

J eff Marrow is the kind of person who comes across as warm, calm and positive, no matter how frustrating the situation. When he tells his story of breaking through to the next level of success, he's so upbeat that it's easy to miss the "hard" parts—those marked by anxiety, worry and disappointment. But they were real.

Jeff started out doing wedding videos, but after two hundred weddings, he decided he'd had enough. There were virtually no repeat clients, so he had to find new business all the time! He

> *"A life without risk is a life without growth."* —David Sandler

started Pattern Productions in 2007 to transition from weddings to professional video production for corporate clients.

He achieved some success as a one-man enterprise and grew his business to six figures in sales, but after five years, he'd hit a wall. He said, "I was getting a lot of interest from new prospective clients. Then they would wrangle me into the 'Let's meet, send me a quote and I'm never going to talk to you again' charade. It was the old run-and-hide act. When I called to follow up, I'd say, 'I sent you the quote and never heard back from you. What's going on?' They'd reply, 'Oh we loved you. You were our second choice.' I heard that too many times. It started driving me crazy."

THE BUYER-SELLER DANCE

Jeff wanted to grow but ran into a constraint in his sales process—it was designed to benefit the buyer. "I needed to grow more and wanted more consistent sales, since I had to provide for my wife and little boy. Somebody would call me and say, 'We have to talk because we need this video right now. It's a huge deal. I've got to have a quote because our CEO wants this video.' Then we would rush to get them a quote and hear nothing back. When we called to follow up, we'd find that it wasn't 'huge' or 'important.' They would say, 'We'll talk to you in two weeks.'"

Jeff was a member of the Entrepreneur Organization's Accelerator group, a mentoring and accountability group for companies on their way to $1 million per year in sales. He told the leader of his group about his challenges in the following terms: "I'm getting in front of people, but they're running and hiding. I give them a quote and then they run off." The leader, who had been through our training, replied, "You need Sandler." Jeff reached out to us, and we decided to begin working together.

His main reason for wanting to work with us? Increasing his income. "I had a viable business," Jeff recalled, "but I wanted to earn more money—not to buy a sports car or a bigger house, but so that I could save more, prepare for the future and have financial security. I was not getting there with my current sales system, and I was stressed. The process was frustrating because of the anxiety I felt. Before every sales call, I asked myself, 'What game are they going to play with me? Are they actually going to buy or not?' I wondered, 'Are they for real? I don't even know what kind of budget they have.' How could I know? At the time I was afraid to bring up the subject of money!"

MONEY ANXIETY

Jeff continued, "My inability to talk about budgets created a lot of anxiety. The prospect would say, 'OK, send us a quote.' Then I'd go back and play all these guessing games with myself. Are they going to be able to afford this or not? Is the quote too high? Am I asking for enough? How could I answer those questions without knowing what they wanted the video for in the first place, how important it was to them and what they were willing to pay for it? I didn't know where their pain was so how could I give them a realistic quote? With the underlying anxiety of keeping the business going, I felt that I needed to win each sale. Soon the sales process became no fun."

The breaking point came after Jeff lost two big opportunities in a row. First, he had a shot at a five-figure deal, which was large for him at the time. He flew up to Chicago on his own money and made a presentation. He thought he had it won because the people at the meeting said they loved his company—and him. In the end, though, they said, "No, we decided to go with somebody else." Jeff told us, "I'd never even discussed competition. I didn't have the training or the guts to ask, 'Are you guys looking at anybody else? What's going to happen when you talk to somebody else? What do you need to hear now to help you understand what we can do?' I never asked questions like that."

Then there was the sales presentation where Jeff met with the client, had a great conversation and thought he'd made a new friend. "It seemed as if he had a good-sized budget," Jeff recalled. "We talked about all sorts of possibilities and I was thinking, *Man, I've got this. This is going to be a winner because this guy likes me.* I went back and did the whole mind game on myself of how to make a quote and sent that over to him. Then he ran and hid. I said to myself, *Not again.* Finally, he got back to me and said, 'We ended up going with this other guy. But you were our second choice.' I'd already heard that again and again. I said to myself, *I'm done*."

A NEW WAY OF SELLING

When Jeff began his training with Sandler, he was ready for a new way of selling. Most students take time to gain comfort with the tools and wait a while to use them. That wasn't Jeff's attitude. From the start, he was in all the way. He called one of our trainers prior to a sales call to discuss the opportunity. He had a meeting with the CEO of a chamber of commerce but had been told that they only had a budget of $2,000 for the shoot. He thought the meeting was a waste of time, especially since he would have to drive an hour to the meeting. His trainer replied, "If you're so busy working on other deals that you don't have time to meet with them, then no, don't do it." Jeff took the meeting.

He recalled, "I went to the meeting thinking that a $2,000 budget was what we were going to discuss. When we started talking, I was asking questions much differently than I had before. I'd been taking the class for a month, so I would draw on paper the Sandler Submarine, a visual representation of the Sandler Selling System, and go through the different steps. When we got to pain, I would take notes on everything that I thought was a pain point and circle them with a 'P.' Since I had driven an hour for the meeting, I decided to talk about money, even if it made me uncomfortable. When we got to the end, I told the client, 'It sounds like you have a budget of $2,000 to make this video.' She said, 'What? $2,000? No, no, no! I didn't talk about $2,000.' I remember that she took her finger, tapped it on the table and said, 'I'm not going to pay more than $1,500 for this video. I think it's ridiculous to spend that kind of money on a video that I'm going to play once.'

"She went into Critical Parent mode, which can be best described as an adult scolding a child. I recognized this right away and I was not going to play along as the child in this interaction. So I backed off. There was a silence in the room. I said, 'I want people to like what we make for them. I want you to be happy with the video. I don't want you to feel like you paid too much for it. If you feel like $2,000 is too much and it's not going to make you happy, then I have a feeling this may not work out. No hard feelings.' I stopped talking. There was silence. Her two administrative assistants were looking down. They didn't even want to make eye contact with me. They couldn't believe that I had said that.

"She sat there for a long time and, the whole time, I expected her to say, 'OK, thanks for coming down.' I was ready to leave. Instead she said, 'Well, what if we...?' And she solved the problem herself. I ended up walking out of there with a $4,000 sale!

"I couldn't believe it. I got that business because I was prepared for the meeting and had gone in there with three kinds of starter questions. I even had an up-front contract that I had written out. Once I was willing to walk away from $1,500, she started talking about what she really needed and we were on an Adult level, rather than Parent to Child. We had a great conversation."

THE BIG MENTAL SHIFT

Jeff had a huge mental shift and started to believe that his training was going to work. He told us, "I realized after that experience that you don't learn things by reading books—you actually need to experience them. That was definitely an existential moment. I said to myself, *I'm going to use the things that I've paid all this money to learn starting right now. This is the time. This is the moment.*"

Jeff had forced out words that made him uncomfortable. He'd been nervous because the prospect was so upset. Nevertheless he made himself be gutsy for a few seconds, and he saw it pay off. Immediately, his perspective changed. He felt so good that he said to himself, *Let's get to the next one!* He had not felt this way in a long, long time. Over the next three months, Jeff sold as much as he had the prior year. He was a man on a mission.

"It kept working. I remember that after every sales call I would walk out and go sit in the car and think, *I can't believe that these things are happening like this.* It was so far from where I was a few months earlier when I left sales meetings thinking, *Now I have to go back and make a quote. I don't know what to do.* I'd walk out of these new meetings knowing what our budget was going to be. For my close I'd review the list of pain points and then ask, 'So if we are able to take care of this and this and this and keep it around this price, what next?' And I'd let them answer. Usually they would say, 'Well, we'll hire you.' That was the close. I just quit talking. Then I'd ask, 'When do you want to start?' We'd pick a date and go."

THE ENTREPRENEUR EMERGES

In less than a year, Jeff became so successful that he merged with another company. He'd become so effective at closing business that he didn't have time to work on production anymore. Soon after the merger, he discovered he was truly an entrepreneur. Unfortunately, with the merger, he'd gone from running his own business his way to working on someone else's terms. Jeff no longer operated under the traditional selling mode. He loved the Sandler methodology because it made him so successful. He was committed to it, but his new company wasn't. Within a year, he decided to leave and start another business. Jeff has now opened a custom letterpress company with his wife.

In his new business, he is learning how to apply the Sandler concepts to a whole different industry. In a business where everyone wants a quote over the phone, Jeff has face-to-face meetings with prospects so he can understand the real issues they're trying to solve. He's reworking his cookbook for a new company, tracking the results and tweaking his plan to what works best.

His advice to other small business owners and salespeople? "If you can just force the difficult, unfamiliar words out of your mouth, do that. I would call my Sandler coach for help, and write down verbatim what I was supposed to say. I learned that I don't have to like doing it—I just have to do it. I had to take a deep breath and say, 'I'm going to say these things.' What's better, asking a tough question or coming in second again? I chose the Sandler way. It was uncomfortable, it was tough, but it has paid off so well."

CHAPTER 12

Letting People Fail

LUCIAN MOREHEAD, CEO
ASTERRA PROPERTIES

L ucian Morehead knew he could sell. His real challenge was building a company. At 23, with an art history degree in one hand and no job prospects in the other, Lucian found himself needing to pay down credit card debt, move back in with his mother and work for his father.

He didn't like that, and before too long he decided to make a change. He'd done some work in real estate. He'd seen how successful many of those who ran commercial real estate companies

> *"Work smart, not hard." —David Sandler*

were. By combining a powerful desire to succeed with an equally powerful fear of failure, he began a long journey of disciplined hard work, determined to make it in the industry.

HITTING THE BOOKS

For the next five months, he spent four to five hours a night, five nights per week, in the local university library. In those pre-Internet days, that was where you went if you were broke and you wanted to study real estate. He soon realized that he needed a crash course in three subjects: business, real estate and selling. He spent three months walking into every real estate office in Austin, Texas, to learn as much as he possibly could about those businesses and the people running them—and maybe, just maybe, he'd get a job offer.

Lucian finally found a paying job doing research for a large real estate outfit, CBRE, and made the princely sum of $1,300 a month. He learned everything he could about the local market: who managed what properties, what occupancies were available and who leased what last. He was still learning, and he was hungry.

A NEW OPPORTUNITY

After fourteen months, Lucian moved into office tenant representation, a service where he would represent tenants by finding and negotiating space for them. In commercial real estate, often senior, more experienced brokers find deals, or transactions, and ask a junior broker to work on the deal with them. The junior broker does the grunt work in an apprenticeship-like role. The fees are then split at the end, sometimes equitably, sometimes not, depending on the firm. The junior brokers can feed themselves two ways: find deals themselves or stay close to senior brokers who have all the deals. Lucian chose to find his own.

He made a commitment to himself: He would walk into a different building every day, learn all he could and call on every single tenant in the building. If he couldn't get a formal meeting with the tenant, he would hang in there and negotiate a short conversation. Using the information from all these meetings, he built a folder of material on every building and every tenant. He did this for 330 multi-tenant buildings in Austin! The larger buildings took as long as three days. Lucian dodged security guards while roaming the halls. Smaller buildings were a little easier; he might knock out two or three of those in a single day.

Gradually, Lucian put together a book of business based on his tireless efforts. He knew whose lease was up and when. He called everyone he could, asking for meetings. If they told him on the phone that they had five years on their lease and he knew it was one or two years, he'd push for a face-to-face meeting. He'd say, "I'm going to be in this business for a long time, and I want to create as many relationships as I can." He found out who the players were in town and got a meeting with everyone he could.

HARD WORK PAYS OFF

"Eventually," he recalled, "I'd covered the entire city, was making tons of calls and calling on the people I knew. I was selling to everybody in my office—all the experienced brokers—because I thought that if they're seeing me work so hard, they're bound to hire me to work on big deals with them. Finally I got to work on a large deal. It was a short-term lease no one else wanted.

"I had faith that my work would pay off. For two and a half years, I took the deals that nobody else wanted. Finally, a high-powered broker noticed my work. She asked me to work on deals with her. She was in another city, but she represented a company that was coming to Austin. She asked me to work on a large deal, and we'd split the commission 50/50. Boom! Now I was working on a big time deal. Soon I became one of the go-to guys for large accounts that were in or coming to Austin: Dell, AT&T, AMD and other national accounts."

A NETWORKING BREAKTHROUGH

During this time, Lucian realized that he could do more deals with less work if he built his network the right way. He'd go to national conventions. He noticed that while other young people partied, the older brokers went to bed and were up early each morning having coffee with brokers from other offices around the world. Lucian followed their lead.

Lucian saw that the successful brokers were building relationships to drive new business. In fact, one of the more seasoned and successful brokers in Lucian's office built his entire book of business by building and working his personal network. Lucian learned two important lessons: 1) He preferred building the relationships with the people he knew rather than with those he didn't; and 2) The people he knew could bring him deals. Those lessons have stuck with him. To this day, he meets people each day for breakfast and lunch as a means of finding business. That's 10 people a week for 50 weeks a year, or 500 new contacts annually.

THE LONG GAME

Lucian began doing more landlord work instead of tenant representation because he wanted fewer, better clients. After six years, he went to work for one of his clients to learn how to put together even more complex deals. He was playing the long game, focusing on where he wanted to go, not just how to make a quick buck today. He briefly set out on his own, but soon realized there was a lot more to learn. He joined another large firm because, he says, "The people there were a lot smarter than I was." Eventually he started his current firm, Asterra Properties, with his partner, Andrew Karr. He'd spent more than fifteen years learning what he calls "the rules of the game." He was experienced in selling, handling a transaction, contracts, letters of intent, credit and cap rates.

Lucian hired two agents and an assistant, but he couldn't teach either agent how to find clients. "They were smart, sharp people with real estate expertise who knew how to handle a transaction, but they didn't know how to go out and get business. I kept having these painful roller coaster rides of 'I'm going to help these agents. Oh gosh! I'm broke! I have to go do deals myself.' I wanted to help them, but that kept me from doing my own deals, and they cost me a lot of money. For two to three years, my partner and I wanted to grow the business. We knew the clients were there. We kept bringing in new brokers, and they kept failing. They were completely dependent on us to bring them business and it was driving us crazy. That's when I picked up the phone and called Sandler.

THE PEOPLE MANAGEMENT CHALLENGE

Lucian was pulling out his hair trying to get his people to do the work necessary to find clients. He realized that he could handle deal management, but people management was different. We spent months with him discussing what was wrong, what was right and how to change the way he worked with brokers.

Lucian recounted, "What I didn't know as an agent, back when I was working for CBRE, was that they had a program for me. I couldn't see the structure and how they did it, because I was in it. With Sandler, we went through an internal belief inventory and learned how they affected selling. We looked at the classic characteristics of a successful 'hunter' profile—someone who's ready to go out, make calls, meet people and get deals. Our agents had a 'doer' profile: 'Tell me what to do and I'll do it.' In the brokerage side of the business you need both types, but if you don't have hunters, you can't keep the doers fed. As we learned the Sandler program, over time we started to see the deficiencies in our people. We figured out which ones were never going to make it in the business unless we just gave them all the clients."

Through Sandler, Lucian and his team learned a selling process that was replicable, something he could hand over to his people. He had unconscious competence when it came to selling, but he couldn't communicate what he knew to his agents. Now he could. He sent all of his people through Sandler training. He found that those who came back to the office talking about the classes became his best producers. The ones who never used it or discussed it struggled or eventually left of their own accord.

What's more, he was learning to manage. He began holding his agents accountable in a different way. Working with Sandler, he learned to uncover their dreams and goals and help them build a plan to turn these into reality. He began meeting with his brokers monthly to review where they were on their business plans and where they needed help. He began holding them more accountable on a daily basis, asking them three questions: "What did you do yesterday? What are you doing today? And are there any areas where you need help?"

Lucian told us, "Once we raised the level of accountability about where they were going, once we asked them whether they were getting there and what happened today, things changed. People either turned things around on their own or they left. When people are failing and not doing what they're supposed to every day, they get it on their own. You don't have to fire them; they just opt out."

IN SEARCH OF THE HUNTER

Lucian began hiring more hunter types. Historically, he had hired based on personality, finding people who could talk "to anyone." That wasn't working out. Using sales-specific assessment tools, he found people who fit a profile that lent itself to proactive hunting. He understood the weaknesses of his people before he hired them and was better able to determine if he wanted to manage those problems.

Lucian said, "We realized that we need people who go after business. That's how our company grows. We'll get our people started by giving them some deals, but we try to spread the wealth. No one's getting 100% of their business from the house, and that forces them to go out and sell. Our program is based off this grass-roots campaign of creating relationships, getting involved and doing good in the community. We aren't necessarily shooting for IBM and Dell Computer type clients, but the reality is that in the last three to four years we've closed huge transactions with Apple and Cigna, companies with big names.

"The moral: Even if we are not focused on large companies, we've found that our relationships will get us into them. That's been a big part of our recent growth. In the last three years, since we've been working with Sandler, we've been able to build our group from 4 agents to 12. We've tripled our size! Even better from my perspective, we've spread our income base from where I brought in 85% of the income to where I'm at 40–50%. Now we've got 50–60% coming from the other people."

LEARNING TO LET PEOPLE FAIL

This growth has led to challenges, and many of those have been personal for Lucian. He wanted to take care of his people, but had to let them fail so they could become self-reliant. As he put it, "I had this real high sense of being an A+ player and not letting anybody down. Too many owners and managers allow their people to develop 'learned helplessness' by rescuing them. That was a big part of our problem. I see now that I'd been doing that for years. I would find the client, do some deals and ask the broker to do some work, but when push came to shove, I would finish it off and close the deal.

"As a result, our people weren't learning as much about closing as they could. Now that's part of their training. I had to put them in a position to fail because that's how you learn. Early on, when I was making all those calls with only a little bit of market knowledge, you wouldn't believe my failure rate. It was off the charts! I failed all the time. But I decided back then that no one was going to hit me for calling them; all they could say was 'no.' I realized I had to let our people reach the same point. I've had to learn how to let our people fail and make themselves more accountable.

"Today there is a different level of connection between the clients and me. We've actually separated a bit, and that's hard if you still want to have relationships with them. It wasn't easy for me, but today the most gratifying sale we make is when somebody brings in a deal that I have never seen, that I don't even know is going on. All of a sudden he walks in with a check. He's getting the lion's share of the proceeds, but our company gets some as well and all we have to do is process the check. That's what I want in our business—I want our people to go out, find the business and transact the business. The sweetest part is seeing our people become successful."

CULTURE SHIFT

Nowadays, Lucian's production as a percentage of company revenue falls every year, and as more people begin producing, the base expands. The company is no longer dependent on Lucian or any other single producer to carry them. The number of transactions the company closes grows every year, which prevents people from spending their time looking for that one elusive "big deal."

The people have changed, but the company culture is still very warm. What's more, the agents doing deals are more proud of their accomplishments than those who were being fed deals three years ago. The mentality has become one of, "I'm going to make it happen," versus believing that the company is responsible for the agent's success.

Lucian adds, "It was a rocky road for a year or two as we let some people go, others chose to leave and new agents joined us. However, as salespeople accept their role and gain the confidence that they can make it happen, it's nothing short of amazing where they can go.

"My goal is to have a company that cares about its people, has good relationships throughout the community, is self-sustaining and can make money. My long-term goal is to spend my time helping agents grow, personally and in their business. It would be great if we make a lot of money, but that's not the most important thing. I want to go home and hang out with my kids. There are a lot of things I want to do besides work. And we keep advancing toward that goal every year."

CHAPTER 13

No Quick Fixes

JULIE SCHATTE, VICE PRESIDENT OF SALES
THE NITSCHE GROUP

J ulie Schatte is a personal case study in the application of this critical Sandler principle: no quick fixes. She found herself in a tough situation that was new to her—sales management— and was able to fake it until she did make it. Her story shows how important it is to have both sales management and members of the sales team following the same system.

The Nitsche Group is a second-generation insurance company headquartered in the small town of Giddings, Texas, population

"You need to fake it until you make it." —David Sandler

5,000, about 50 miles northeast of Austin. Julie has been with the company for 21 years. Over that time she has seen it grow from 23 to 126 employees, more than a fivefold increase.

Julie started out in sales at first, spending her first seven years on the inside and then three years selling both inside and outside. Her job gradually evolved into a marketing position tasked with generating leads and creating brand awareness, but Julie was still expected to produce some sales. Since Julie had no experience in marketing, she did some research and adapted the best practices of her peers in the industry.

After successfully running the marketing department for 10 years, Julie began her transformation into a sales manager role. This is the role in which she faced her greatest challenge.

Generally there are two ways someone can be put into a leadership position. The first option is simply an announcement from the senior leadership stating that this person is now in charge. The other option is by osmosis. It happens when the person naturally evolves into the leadership position by slowly and deliberately taking on more responsibility. The latter is how Julie evolved into the sales manager job. She wanted to grow—not settle for where she was—and she was constantly looking for ways to take on more responsibility. She wanted to prove something to herself and others. By doing administrative tasks for the sales department, generating reporting metrics and organizing the department, she eventually found herself with the title "Sales Manager."

The promotion was rare both in her office and in the male-dominated insurance industry. Women often have important positions in insurance, but it's much more common for them to make contributions behind the scenes. To actually manage a team of productive salespeople? Almost unheard of for a woman in a small Texas town!

THE JOB SHE WANTED

Although Julie has an incredible work ethic and an unsurpassed desire to learn, she was not prepared for what sales management threw at her.

For one thing, even though this was the job she wanted, she was not trained in advance on how to coach, mentor, motivate, recruit and, ultimately, hold salespeople accountable. To further complicate matters, she inherited a team made up of two groups: veterans who had built a solid book of business, and others who had been there for many years but who were not performing up to expectations. Adding to these difficult dynamics was the fact that her firm was in the midst an ongoing leadership transition, from the founding generation to the next generation of ownership. Julie was inheriting a leadership role in a company with a very complex culture. The sales team required a strong leader willing to make tough choices and fundamental changes.

As a side note, we should point out that the single most

common problem we see in sales organizations is the way the sales management position is filled. Far too often senior leadership simply promotes the top performing salesperson to sales manager based on the false assumption that such superstars can somehow replicate themselves. This is an unrealistic expectation with no measurable evidence to back it up. It's like assuming that a top quarterback in the NFL can take over the job of head coach without the years of training and experience needed to be successful in a vastly different role.

In nearly 100% of the cases that we have seen, new sales managers are not adequately trained, or not trained at all, in the leadership and management disciplines that this difficult job requires. As a result, the company ends up losing a good salesperson and gains an ineffective sales manager. It's the Peter Principle at work: "In a hierarchy, every employee tends to rise to his or her own level of incompetence." Julie broke that rule, though—by developing new competencies and a new way of looking at herself.

"NO IDEA WHAT I WAS GETTING INTO"

We've been working with Julie for about three years now. From the beginning she was extremely open about sharing her story with us. She is very passionate and committed to succeeding, and it shows whenever she talks about her job, whether in person or on the phone. She told us, "When I took over the sales manager position my internal dialogue was that if I am not the right person, I would quickly step aside. I wanted to give my president the assurance that I could admit failure and move on." We had no idea that she was harboring this internal script.

She said, "I was so afraid that I would fail that I began to obsess about how I would pull off this move. Looking back, I had no idea what I was getting into. There were no systems of accountability. Some long-term sales representatives needed to move on—after 10 years on the job they were still not producing. Some of them were friends and former peers, which made things much more difficult.

"In addition, I had multiple reporting relationships with far too many people to keep happy. There was no CRM. A typical coaching call with a salesperson went something like this: 'What did you sell?' At the same time, the owner was making plans to acquire other agents and rapidly expand the company. The entire situation was overwhelming, and I was intimidated.

"I must admit that in the heat of the battle, I acted defensively under all that pressure. I didn't want people to know that I was not 100% confident in what I was doing. Despite my best efforts, I was not an effective leader because I was obsessed with keeping everyone happy. The team saw that and, as a result, I did not have their respect."

A LIFE OUT OF BALANCE

"I could see that this pressure was having a negative impact on my personal life," Julie continued. "I was quickly becoming out of balance. I wouldn't even stop to have lunch with the staff; instead

I worked through lunch at my desk. I would do whatever it took, but all my efforts were not enough.

"I was working more than 60 hours a week and taking work home at night and on weekends. Worst of all, I wasn't fully there for my husband and children, since I couldn't stop focusing on my new job. My biggest fear was that I was giving my children the wrong impression of what 'success' looked like. I didn't want my driven, compulsive behavior to happen to them!

"Then, my president signed me up for a sales management course with Sandler. I'd never heard of Sandler and was not happy at having to lose time from work. All I could think about was that the training would require me to make a two-hour round trip to attend the classes, plus class time and homework. I wondered how I was going to fit this into my already crowded schedule. Even before my first session, I found I was becoming more stressed. I told myself, 'This can't possibly help.'

"I couldn't have been more wrong about Sandler. After a few months in the program, I realized that Sandler was giving me the structure that I needed to start the process of getting things under control. The training made it clear that we needed a unified sales process to meet the growth objectives of our president and the management disciplines to drive that change.

"I made the decision that my first step would be to work on myself. One of the most powerful lessons was I/R Theory. I needed to separate my identity as a person from my role as a manager. I worked on convincing myself that I could be imperfect and that was OK. I started to change my original self-limiting negative message of, 'How am I going to pull this off?' to 'What do I need to do to get this done?' That was a big change for me."

USING THE TOOLS

"The Sandler communication tools gave me more awareness of the people I worked with and what makes them tick," Julie said. "Slowly I started to gain confidence in my decisions and my vision. I realized that understanding people would become a way of life from now on. First, I made adjustments in my relationship with my husband, and they have been beneficial for us.

"Next, I have a daughter who's going off to college soon. I realized that I had a tendency to revert to the judgmental Critical Parent ego state with her when we communicated. For example, she texted me one day at work about meeting a boyfriend and my immediate reaction was to text back in that Critical Parent voice. Only this time, I heard myself!

"As I drove home, I thought about the interaction with my daughter and how my stepfather had treated me the same way. In the past, I would have let the incident with my daughter blow over. However, when I got home I did something different. I took responsibility for my actions and explained to my daughter why I acted the way I did. I also told her the changes I would make to help our conversations take place in the Adult ego state.

"As a result of my own self-development, I now have a heightened sense of awareness about how I make others feel. I can catch myself when I'm acting in a non-productive manner. I also have the ability to change my behavior on the fly and the guts to go back and correct the issue later if that is what's needed."

DEVELOPING THE TEAM

"Once I started to get myself in order," Julie told us, "I turned my focus toward the development of the sales team. They needed to get competent in Sandler, and I knew that they would fight that process hard. I needed to implement a CRM system. I had to have a structured onboarding process in place for the wave of new people who would soon be reporting to me. I needed behavioral data for analytics. I knew we could no longer afford to 'wing it' based on gut feeling. Sandler gave me the confidence to take action and deal with these issues.

"I also had to let some people go, which was very difficult given our long relationship and that some were close friends. However, it had to be done. I bit the bullet and made the proper personnel changes. I have to say, it was a great relief.

"In replacing these long-time employees, I had faced two key issues: my need for approval, and the fact that some of the people I let go were peers. I had a lot of worries. If I fired them, would they go around me and ask for reinstatement? Here's how I dealt with that. Instead of asking for senior management's approval, I carefully explained to management why these team members were not in the right positions, told management what I was going to do and proceeded to do it. Management supported me completely.

I now have the confidence to assert myself professionally. The former team members were good people, but they were not in the right jobs given all the changes we were making. I believe that all parties were better off when we parted company."

HANDLING RESISTANCE

Julie had more to say about the process: "As we started to train the sales team, I experienced all kinds of resistance. They were accustomed to short-term, flavor-of-the-month sales training that they wouldn't be held accountable for using, even though I explained to them that the primary Sandler Training principle was long-term reinforcement.

"This was not a quick fix but a lifetime change of attitude and behavior. Every time they pushed back about the training, I had the same short message to meet their resistance: 'How can this not help you?' Once they saw the consistency and conviction in my message, I slowly started to gain their support.

"Now the team's behaviors are starting to improve and they are beginning to buy in. Our Sandler trainer explained to me the amount of time that it typically takes to change the culture of a sales organization. I accepted that our problems did not manifest themselves in a year, and they wouldn't be fixed in a year, either."

A CHANGE IN LEADERSHIP STYLE

Julie learned a lot herself. "The biggest professional impact I've gotten from Sandler is the change in my leadership style. Instead of being defensive, I now encourage people to share their issues with me. I don't take things personally as I did when I was afraid of being exposed as an inexperienced leader. This change may sound simple, but it took a lot of introspection and re-programming of my beliefs.

"Recently, those changes were put to the test. I had a major conflict with another long-time coworker. My normal tendency would be to win at all costs. I soon realized that winning would get me nowhere. I used the Sandler tools to help me deal with the conflict by lowering my emotional involvement, seeking help from my peers and dealing with the conflict in a calm and confident manner. We handled the issue effectively and unemotionally. I kept my self-respect and earned the respect of my coworker.

"I am a huge fan of the Sandler communication tools and I can't say enough about their impact on our organization. We have only had our sales team with Sandler for a few months now, but already I can see the difference in their attitudes, communication and how they pursue deals. The big payoff will be in the next two years as the entire culture turns over.

"I believe Sandler Training will make a difference in all aspects of the company, including our internal and external communication. My confidence in Sandler led to having more than a hundred of our other employees trained in Sandler's Strategic Customer Care course. My expectation is that the entire company will reach a new level of productivity because there will be more efficient communication, less conflict and better teamwork."

As we concluded our interview with Julie, we felt proud of the way she took the initiative to make necessary internal changes. By developing herself first, she demonstrated to others in the company how change could make a difference. Her own growth allowed her to take control of the sales organization with authority. Now that they have a functional leader, her sales team is on track to grow consistently.

CHAPTER 14

One Thing at a Time

MATT WILCOXSON, VICE PRESIDENT, STRATEGIC SALES
DRILLINGINFO

W e first met Matt Wilcoxson in a small, overstuffed conference room in Houston during the kick-off boot camp
for Drillinginfo's sales team. Matt had been selling for
about two years. He is quiet and unassuming, and at first you
never knew where you stood with him. But his responses were
right on the money, so we knew that he was engaged.

> *"You can't lose anything that you don't have."* —David Sandler

A CAREER CHANGE

After graduating from the University of Texas with a degree in urban and regional development, Matt started his career as a real estate consultant. He oversaw big multi-use projects and quickly realized that he enjoyed selling the project more than managing it. Matt decided that consulting and managing large projects with long-term completion dates was not what he wanted to do with his career. He grew up around the oil and gas industry and was always intrigued by it. Drillinginfo, which supplies intelligence and data for energy exploration and production companies, offered him the opportunity to join an industry he was excited about and work in sales, an area that was starting to interest him. People had often told him that he should be in sales, but until he got that job offer he had steered away from selling.

Matt landed that sales position with Drillinginfo without a resume, experience or a formal interview. As the story goes, Matt's roommate Colin joined Drillinginfo first. Colin then went to work hard on Matt as he tried to talk him into joining the company. Colin told Matt that Drillinginfo was specifically looking for young, eager, inexperienced salespeople to train and grow as the company grew.

It took about a month before Matt seriously considered making the move to Drillinginfo. He declined the early offers because having known Colin for so long, Matt believed that his friend was often overly optimistic. In this case, however, Colin's hunch was right, and Matt's caution was unnecessary. The two of them still joke about it.

The early days, however, were challenging. After a short time in the position, Matt became acutely aware of the situation he faced. He was with a small startup company competing head to head with a huge publicly traded company that dominated the industry. This was a true "David and Goliath" matchup. As if that weren't enough, he knew little about the software platform that he was selling. The job was a challenging one: Matt had to sell software subscriptions to oil drilling companies in an industry staffed with seasoned professionals who had little time for "a kid who's not from the oil patch."

We asked Matt if he felt any remorse following his move into sales. "Yes," he said. "I did—from the first cold call to the first *no* there was plenty of self-doubt. The *no* was crippling, and it was followed quickly by another. As they piled up, I was getting more frustrated by the day. My biggest bout of low self-confidence came when the company asked me to move to Denver and open a brand-new territory. We had a tiny client base but huge expectations. I didn't know a soul in Denver, and I had very little support at the time. The first day of work was a real eye opener for me. I was essentially on my own with very few resources, but I had big goals to achieve. It was terrifying at times, but the excitement of being in a new city and a new position, with a bright path ahead of me, overcame those moments of doubt."

GOING IT ALONE

Before he started working with Sandler, Matt's only sales training had been the mentoring he received from a coworker who was the only veteran salesperson in the company. There were no other trained salespeople in the entire organization.

Matt was continually frustrated by the long sales cycle that had become widespread within the company. This was due to the fact that the initial subscription had been rolled out at a low price point to build a user base as quickly as possible. As time went by, the users fell in love with the technology. Drillinginfo spent a lot of money on developing the platform. The price had to be raised substantially to cover the company's increased investments in improving technology—and some customers got an increase that was two to five times what they had been paying.

Although the competition was still far more expensive and Matt had a superior product, buyers constantly pushed back at the mention of any price increase. In fact many became angry and made Matt's sales calls quite difficult. This proved to be quite a challenge for a young guy new to the industry.

When Matt called on clients to renew at the new price level, he was faced with a long list of objections and the reality that budgets were continually tightening with the economic crash. Often Matt would hear, "What's changed so much that you are asking us to pay twice as much, if not more?" Yet he typically got this complaint from procurement groups, not from the people who actually used the product and knew the positive impact it had. Clients and prospects in procurement actually told Matt that they didn't care what kind of impact it had on their organization.

EXECUTING A GROWTH STRATEGY—BY SELF-EVALUATING

Allen Gilmer, the CEO and founder of Drillinginfo, hired Sandler Training to develop and grow the sales organization. Allen's vision was to build a world-class sales team by training all the salespeople to use the same sales methodology. He envisioned a team that could execute his growth strategy while setting the foundation for much faster expansion. We kicked off the training program with a two-day boot camp, followed by a year of ongoing weekly reinforcement. The boot camp was Matt's first exposure to the Sandler selling methodology.

When Matt was assessed for his selling abilities, the findings were not the strongest on the team. He was rated as "weak" in several areas, such as handling the money conversation, questioning strategies and not following a structured sales process.

The assessment results could have frustrated many salespeople, but they only served to fuel Matt's desire to become successful. He viewed the results as information and did not take them personally.

CHANGING COURSE

Matt realized that the first tough change he had to make was his ability to establish real rapport. He told us, "Prior to the training, I thought that bonding and rapport was having beers, talking and socializing, while trying to be liked. The people I was selling to were really tough on me, so my strategy was to defuse criticism by getting them to like me. That was the wrong strategy and only led to a longer sales cycle and a lot of wasted energy on my part.

"I realized that I had to change the way I interacted with people. I worked hard to train myself that talking to potential clients did not mean that I was building rapport with them. I had to rely on other subtle aspects of building rapport, such as active listening, maintaining prospects' OK-ness, matching and mirroring, and identifying their communication style. If I failed to establish rapport, why would prospects ever tell me the truth on a call? If they didn't tell me the truth, how would I know if we could really help them?"

BEYOND FACTS AND LOGIC

When asked about his strategy for handling the significant price increase before learning Sandler principles, Matt responded, "I was over-presenting with too many features and benefits in the hope of convincing people with facts and logic. Looking back, I realize I was far more worried about the price increase than the client was. I was afraid to walk away, mistakenly thinking that if I never heard the word 'no,' there was a chance that I could get the deal done later. I kept telling prospects what I thought they wanted to hear. As a result, I was making no effort to ask prospects what they wanted.

"The peak of my frustration came in 2009 when the markets crashed. Now the buyers had a real excuse not to pay more, and I was out of ways to overcome that objection.

"A turning point for me came on a call I was afraid to make. I was expecting to get my head handed to me from a prospect who had the reputation for being difficult and was with a $4 billion company. As soon as I walked in and sat down, the prospect said in a stern voice, 'I have no idea how you can help us. I probably should have not set this meeting.' After months of frustration chasing long sales cycles, being misled and being disrespected, I got out of my seat and said politely, 'Then maybe we shouldn't meet.' The prospect looked at me and said, 'Hold on a second, where are you going?' To which I replied, 'You said that you didn't want to meet.'

"I was not expecting what happened next, even though I had heard about this outcome time and time again in Sandler classes. The prospect said, 'Sit down, son,' and a candid, in-depth conversation followed. The prospect soon revealed that he had previously invested over $1 million in a legacy system that wasn't working. It became vividly clear to me that he needed my solution to save that large investment. I could not believe that he shared this information with me because it was so personal. At last, I understood the source of his real pain and how I could fix it. In the end, he renewed with far more options and signed the contract at five times the current price. It all happened because I got tired of dealing with people beating me up. I have rights on a sales call, and one of those rights is to be treated with respect.

"After the call, I headed back to my car and sat down. I sighed, and then I smiled. I had had fun on that call and could not wait to do it again! All I had to do was be brave for five seconds at a time.

"Before I started working with Sandler, I was frustrated and near my emotional breaking point. I did not see any alternative to backed-up sales pipelines and having to deal with nasty prospects over and over again. Once I saw how Sandler worked, I knew I had an out. Until then, I perceived a lost sale as a personal failure. That misperception was killing me. Looking back, I have to laugh at the self-limiting beliefs I was carrying."

SELLING WITH A PURPOSE

Matt continued, "As I learned more about Sandler, I decided to apply bits and pieces of the system to deal with the most common problems I faced in the field. I recall talking with my manager about my rate of improvement. As he coached me, he asked me to focus on getting 3% better each month and to do one thing at a time, as opposed to trying to fix everything at once. This slow and steady process allowed me to deploy tactics individually and gradually become more comfortable with them.

"I see sales as a very tough career if you don't change your outlook. I decided to act self-confident, sell with a sense of purpose and move beyond conventional selling. I don't see traditional sales as a meaningful career. Conventional salespeople push products and services, and they don't really believe in what they're doing at a deep personal level. With Sandler, the selling actually became meaningful to me. Why? There is a deeper connection with the prospect when you use Sandler. If the Sandler process is followed, the salesperson is presenting the best possible solution to a fully qualified prospect—a solution that is in the prospect's best interest. If there is a fit, lives and careers are changed. Of course that means something."

When asked if he had any closing advice, Matt replied, "The Sandler sales process can be easy to learn, especially if you are open-minded and commited to making the necessary internal changes. You will have to reframe some of your internal beliefs, and that takes time and can be difficult. For example, I thought that I could never confront a prospect. I had to change that belief to one that sounds like, 'It's OK to confront a prospect, if I am nurturing them while doing so.' It's been a great journey. When I started with Sandler seven years ago, I was only selling about $250,000 a year. This year I will be involved with leading a team responsible for over $15 million in revenue. Sandler works!"

PART THREE:

The Road from Here

You've just finished a collection of stories about ordinary people who have done some extraordinary things, not only in their businesses, but also in their larger experience as individuals committed to personal growth. They saw their companies grow. They personally reaped a large windfall. Most importantly, though, they changed their lives. If you lead salespeople or sell yourself, you have the same choice: Continue with the status quo, or pursue your own breakthrough—and succeed the Sandler way.

The question everyone asks about breakthroughs is, "How do I do this?" There are no short, easy answers because changing our behaviors and attitudes is a difficult process. It requires more time than our society usually wants to tolerate. People want quick fixes. We at Sandler don't tout quick fixes, but rather a

"There is no emotional growth when you're procrastinating" —David Sandler

reinforcement-based approach. First and foremost, we encourage you to seek out a Sandler trainer yourself.

You can take steps on your own right now to create a breakthrough. Consider beginning with the following.

Take some time to become clear on your professional and personal intentions. What are you passionate about? Where do you want to go? What do you want to accomplish? For what do you want to be known? Then ask "why" for each of your answers. You have to know your "whys" before you can sincerely commit to making an effective change in your thoughts and actions.

Inventory your own challenges. Write down everything that is holding you back from breaking through to the next level. Then, go through and cross out all items that are out of your control; i.e., "The stock market is down right now." After you've inventoried your problems, determine which are attitude problems, which are issues of behavior and which are challenges with your selling or management techniques.

Identify and re-script your negative attitudes. For instance, if you believe your sales cycle is too long, re-script that with something more supportive, such as, "I can close deals quickly." If you feel you aren't worth talking to, you can re-script that with, "I could be the most important conversation for someone today."

Help yourself out mentally and emotionally by reinforcing these messages constantly.

For your behavior and technique challenges, build an action plan you can commit to for a short period of time, such as 30 days. Commit to those actions until they become habit.

Most importantly, keep a journal of your attitudes and behaviors. Identify self-limiting beliefs you have on sales calls, in business and with coworkers, employers and employees. Chart your behavior on a daily basis to note which activities lead to success and which are a waste of time. Ask yourself after sales or management encounters, "What did I do well? What could I have done better?" Have the guts to be honest with yourself about the answers.

Lastly, we recommend reading, and rereading, *Accountability the Sandler Way*, by Hamish Knox.

This is only the beginning, but it's a crucial first step: Understand where you are and where you want to go. Deepen your understanding on that and what needs to happen for you to get there. Everyone in this book, including the authors, made a decision to change his or her thoughts and actions. We all took responsibility for our own lives and results. The only way for change to happen was for each of us to look inside, honestly assess ourselves and make a change. If we can, you can, too. We wish you the best of luck—and good selling.

APPENDIX

Common Limiting Beliefs

E ach person in the book shared some examples of their self-limiting beliefs. Everyone has some self-limiting beliefs—that's normal. Many are very successful at burying these beliefs deep inside their subconscious so they are hardly aware of them.

Having training thousands of sales leaders and salespeople, we can make a list of the most common self-limiting beliefs. Many of these beliefs have no adverse impact on our lives—except when we find ourselves in a sales process! Take a moment to scan the list of the most common self-limiting beliefs below. If you carry around even one of these beliefs, it's too expensive. We recommend taking action by seeing a Sandler trainer.

Please note, these beliefs can vary in intensity, and you may not use these precise words in your internal dialogue with yourself. Think of the following as broad categories of limiting belief.

1. I don't like sales—it's not an admirable profession.

2. I am only a salesperson—no one really wants to talk to me.

3. I am uncomfortable admitting to people that I am a salesperson.

4. I don't feel as if I am a peer with the prospect on the sales call.

5. The prospect holds all the power during the sales process.

6. It's not appropriate to confront the prospect.

7. I feel bad (or beat myself up) when I lose a deal—it's my fault.

8. Buyers are always honest with me, so I should never question them.

9. Prospects can get under my skin and annoy me.

10. When I am asked a question, I must answer it right away.

11. It's not appropriate to ask about the prospect's money and finances.

12. I am uncomfortable talking about money—it's not polite.

13. I am uncomfortable asking for access to other people in higher positions.

14. I prefer calling lower in the organization first.

15. I close deals with a great presentation—no matter how much higher we are in price than the competition.

16. I don't want to look or feel pushy under any circumstances.

17. It's normal for the prospect to think it over or to shop my proposal.

18. I must have the best price to close deals.

19. My industry is different.

20. I really don't need a formal sales process—I can get by on my instincts.

Make your own list of self-limiting beliefs to analyze.

Now ask yourself: "If I were to effectively replace these self-limiting beliefs with more productive beliefs, what would happen?" Sandler Training can help you find out.

Look for these other books
on shop.sandler.com:

Prospect the Sandler Way

Transforming Leaders the Sandler Way

Selling Professional Services the Sandler Way

Accountability the Sandler Way

Selling Technology the Sandler Way

LinkedIn the Sandler Way

Bootstrap Selling the Sandler Way

Customer Service the Sandler Way

Selling to Homeowners the Sandler Way

CONGRATULATIONS!

Succeed the Sandler Way

includes a complimentary seminar!

Take this opportunity to personally experience the non-traditional sales training and reinforcement coaching that has been recognized internationally for decades.

Companies in the Fortune 1000 as well as thousands of small- to medium-sized businesses choose Sandler for sales, leadership, management, and a wealth of other skill-building programs. Now, it's your turn, and it's free!

You'll learn the latest practical, tactical, feet-in-the-street sales methods directly from your neighborhood Sandler trainers! They're knowledgeable, friendly and informed about your local selling environment.

Here's how you redeem YOUR FREE SEMINAR invitation.

1. Go to www.Sandler.com and click on Find Training Location (top blue bar).
2. Select your location.
3. Review the list of all the Sandler trainers in your area.
4. Call your local Sandler trainer, mention *Succeed the Sandler Way* and reserve your place at the next seminar!